Food for Hezron

Duke Hammond

ISBN 978-1-0980-5845-6 (paperback)
ISBN 978-1-0980-5846-3 (digital)

Copyright © 2020 by Duke Hammond

All rights reserved. No part of this publication may be reproduced, distributed, or transmitted in any form or by any means, including photocopying, recording, or other electronic or mechanical methods without the prior written permission of the publisher. For permission requests, solicit the publisher via the address below.

Christian Faith Publishing, Inc.
832 Park Avenue
Meadville, PA 16335
www.christianfaithpublishing.com

Printed in the United States of America

Dedication

Lindsey, your mom is the strongest of four sisters who are strong in many ways. I speak of her physical strength. All of them exhibit commitment to tasks and exemplary moral character. You come from good stock. My prayer for you is that you will realize you have the potential to be great. You have a formidable opponent. It has a ferocious grip. But it is helpless against the Creator of the universe and His Son, Jesus.

The little boy in this true story needed help to survive. God gave that help not so much for the little boy but for you. Yes, you Lindsey.

How I wonder what He has in store for your life!

The southwest coast of the big island of Hawaii below Mauna Loa volcano is one of the most beautiful places I've seen on earth. There's a coffee plantation there run by a hardworking woman named "Patty." Maybe you could go there and help her. Just a thought. I'll bet she'd love to have you. Free room and board too. You can call her mom.

Love you,
Uncle Duke

Acknowledgements

Candy, no words are adequate. Thank you for my office. Thank you for understanding that thinking takes time. I'd have preferred spending it with you but I had to obey His call. You're the best! Thank you for the "push" I needed to undertake this.

Suzanne, Beth, Jo, and Ann—your encouragement meant more than you know. What Godly daughters with Christian husbands and eleven baptized believers as children. Your testimonies allow me to comfortably sit and write.

Becky, I don't understand your gift but I'm certain it's real. When I was first thinking of writing, you bravely said you "saw" me writing and God "told" you to tell me that's what God wanted. That gave me the confirmation I needed to step away from nearly fifty years of teaching Bible to do this. Thank you for your bravery.

Pastor Rob, thank you for accepting my leaving teaching and joining my class with yours. When you hadn't "heard" from the Lord about it but trusted that I had, made it easy on me.

Lauren and Jonnie, I know you both think you did little to help me but that just illustrates how technically inept I am. Thank you both for the help I needed to continue along this path. May the Lord repay you both.

Finally, to all the staff at Christian Faith Publishing, a huge Thank You! Thank you Valerie for explaining the process so clearly and making what seemed to me an impossibility become a reality. Thank you Megan for coordinating production, editing, page and cover design and all the staff that had a role…what talented people you all are!

Preface

How could anyone be so presumptuous to believe they could add anything of value to what Moses, while inspired by the Holy Spirit, wrote about Joseph? I am certainly not so presumptuous. But what I've written is less about Joseph and more about you. I believe I am qualified to write about you because I suspect you're very much like me.

You probably don't feel inclined to read a book about Jacob's son Joseph. You think you know all you need to know about him already. Perhaps you do. But do you know what God is saying to you about you in the story of Joseph? I taught the story of Joseph's life for years before I discovered what God was saying to me.

This book might serve as a shortcut for you. If you discover what God wants you to understand about your relationship with Him by examining the circumstances of Joseph's life, it will improve yours.

Are there problems that trouble you in life? Does life seem unfair? Does your life sometimes appear to be a hopeless jumble of totally unrelated events? Perhaps your life is more like an endless boring routine. Is that monotonous rut in which you travel getting deeper? Do you cry out to God for deliverance and hear no answer?

Read this book. God wants to change your life!

Introduction

"What's this?" asks Jacob.

"Is this your son's coat or not?" answer ten of his sons.

"It is my son's coat, an evil beast hath devoured him; Joseph is without doubt rent in pieces," Jacob cries (Genesis 37:33).

Our lives are shattered in seconds. We often imagine a future with no laughter after experiencing tragedy. We lack understanding. We have no vision. Our hope is gone. Worse, we believe we are responsible for our lost happiness. An even greater mistake is misconstruing God's blessings as punishments and even reasons for suicide!

Have you met many people who have problem-free lives? No? Me either. Life is full of trouble. No one is exempt. While living through problems is never fun, we actually become more resilient to life's difficulties by having experienced them.

You see, we tend to equate God's loving us with His giving us problem-free lives. When that doesn't happen, we fear He really doesn't care about us. We pray, get no answers, and give up. We aren't mad at God, but we cease to "bother" Him with what bothers us. We trek through life, suffering as we go.

If this is you, it's time for a wake-up call! *Food for Hezron* can give the most miserable of Christian's hope. My prayer is that you will read it, do the daily studies, and develop a stronger faith in God's love for you.

God doesn't desire to show any of us how or why He works. He desires us to become people of faith who trust Him despite life's difficult circumstances. Your belief in that principle will determine your effectiveness as a warrior for Christ. While that may not be your desire, scripture is clear…it is what God wants! (Ephesians 6:10–18).

Chapter 1

In the eighteenth century BC, there was a family living near Mount Hebron, 2,800 feet above sea level, twenty miles west of the Dead Sea. The family consisted of a husband, one of his two wives (one wife had died giving birth to his twelfth son), his wives' two handmaids, and twelve sons of those four women. The husband's name was Jacob (Genesis 37:1).

Long before he was married, Jacob was asked by his father to speak his true name. He lied (Genesis 27:18–19). He lied in order to receive a blessing from his father that rightly belonged to his older twin brother, Esau. Jacob's father was fooled by the trick as he was old and had lost his sight (Genesis 27:1). The lie Jacob told led to the breakup of his family and a long estrangement from his brother.

More than twenty years later (Genesis 31:38), Jacob was about to come into the company of his brother, Esau, for the first time since that breakup (Genesis 32:6). Jacob was certain Esau would still want to kill him as he had spoken when they parted (Genesis 27:41–42). On the eve of that reunion until the breaking of the day, Jacob wrestled with a being who did not identify himself (Genesis 32:24). We learn from the prophet Hosea (Hosea 12:4) that Jacob had wrestled with an angel who was a messenger from God. These many years, Jacob had been living as though he were Esau. Jacob's father had given him Esau's blessing because of this deception. Jacob had been enjoying a life enriched by a blessing he had stolen from Esau. God hadn't forgotten! For more than twenty years, God had watched Jacob living a lie.

While Jacob wrestled, he threatened to hold the angel until the angel blessed him. It is so interesting that instead of simply refusing, the angel demands that Jacob identify himself (Genesis 32:27).

He says, "What is thy name?" Remember, the last time Jacob had been asked that question, he had lied. What would he say now? God wanted to know. Sometimes we get second chances. Jacob responds, "Jacob." God says, "Thy name shall be called no more Jacob but Israel…" (Genesis 32:28). We now have the birth of the nation of Israel.

Sins are often repeated in subsequent generations of families. Psychologists tell us that children who are abused by their parents often commit the same on their own children. This happens often in our experience, and here is a Biblical example. Isaac had favored Esau. Isaac's wife, Rebekah, had favored Jacob (Genesis 25:28). Favoritism contributed to the destruction of Isaac's family. Rebekah orders her favorite son, Jacob, to stay "a few days" with her brother to keep Jacob safe from Esau. "A few days" turns into 7,300 days (Genesis 31:38), and what's more, Rebekah never again sees Jacob on this earth.

Now the last person you might expect to see committing the sin of favoritism is Jacob. He had seen it pit him against his brother, cause him to lie to his father, and separate him from his mother in this life. But by the time we learn of Joseph's early life, we find that he too is a victim of favoritism committed by Jacob (Genesis 37:3).

Sons of mothers who are battered by their husbands often batter their own wives in later life. Think about your own memories of childhood. Can you remember actual words spoken to you by your parents? Probably not unless those words were often repeated sayings, but you can undoubtedly remember specific "things" your parents did. Parents need to realize their children learn far more from watching their parent's behavior than from hearing what their parents say. Well, so did Jacob (Exodus 34:6–7). Jacob raised his sons the same way he was raised.

In Genesis 37:1, we find Israel (Jacob) dwelling in what would become the promised land. But Jacob doesn't realize that his family is the nation of Israel or that they currently occupy the place where Joshua would lead the nation of Israel several hundred years later. The family lives on the northern slopes of Mount Hebron. Joseph is seventeen years old, and his younger brother Benjamin is the last born of twelve brothers.

Joseph was loved more than his other brothers by his father, Israel, (Genesis 37:3). Israel made this obvious to the older brothers by keeping Joseph at home when he was certainly old enough to be working with his brothers as a shepherd and also by giving him a beautiful coat of many colors unlike any of his brother's clothes. It may come as no surprise that Joseph's brothers hated him (Genesis 37:4).

Here is a great lesson for us all. Few friends and fewer siblings derive much pleasure from our good fortune when it comes at their expense. Can you imagine giving a present to your child on one of your other children's birthdays and not giving a gift to the child whose birthday it was? Who could do such a thing? Jacob did. Joseph's brothers hated him. They also had little respect for their father as we shall see.

There are no sins recorded in scripture attributed to Joseph. We will discuss why that is later. It certainly can't be due to the possibility that he never sinned (Romans 3:10, 23). Joseph did have one or two character flaws however. He seemed to be naive and also lacked tact. After dreaming he would one day rule over his mother, father, and brothers, he shares this with them in the ultimate act of simplicity (Genesis 37:5–11). What could he have been thinking? Did he expect them all to believe it might happen and rejoice with him about it? If his announcement wasn't a sin, it was certainly tactless and naive. But you must admit it was honest. Unthinking perhaps, but honest.

In Genesis 37:12, Joseph's brothers traveled about forty-eight miles north to graze the flock in Shechem. Israel then calls Joseph and asks him to go ninety-six miles round trip just to check up on his brothers.

Now just think about that for a moment in the context of our lives today. You have one son working outside and another inside, reading a book. I say reading a book because I hope he isn't wasting his time playing a video game or watching television. You ask your son who's reading the book to stop, put the book down, and go out and check on the other son to see how the work is going. How would your book-reading son react? Now what if your working son was a quarter of a mile away on your farm? What if he was on the other side of your town if you live in one? How about if he was forty-eight miles somewhere north of you in open country, grazing your farm animals?

I know the answer to those questions, and so do you. I brought up my children with Christian values in a Christian home. They are wonderful Christians today, and they were a pleasure to live with when they were under my authority. But my book-reading son would have let me know with facial expressions and body language that checking on his brother in the backyard was an inconvenience. Traveling a quarter mile across my farm would have at least resulted in a request to reconsider. Going across town would have resulted in an argument. And traveling forty-eight miles somewhere north would have resulted in a blank stare conveying the thought, *Dad's gone crazy!*

Don't be too quick to dismiss your son's probable behavior with "times are different now." I know they are. But children shouldn't be. Anyway, what I really want you to grasp is that Joseph is different!

Seventeen hundred years or so, after Joseph, Jesus is asked by His Father to do a difficult thing. He goes to the cross willingly to die there in pain for you. The Old Testament is filled with "types" of Christ. These types all illustrate some aspect of the Messiah's work. Why just in Genesis we have the ark of Noah. There was only one door, and you had to be in the ark to be saved (Genesis 6:16). We also have Melchizedek, king of Salem (Peace), the priest of the most high God to whom Abraham paid tithes (Genesis 14:18). There was a ram caught in a thicket that became a substitute sacrifice for Isaac (Genesis 22:13). And now we have Joseph who is a perfect type of Christ. The Bible records no sins for Joseph. He had them of course, but scripture doesn't record them. And now Joseph obeys his father in a difficult task. No back talk, bad facial expressions, or body language, just "here am I" (Genesis 37:13). Jacob sent him, and he went. Christ goes to the cross as His Father bid Him. It is a difficult trip, but Christ says in effect, "Here am I." That Joseph is a type of Christ will become even more obvious in the rest of his story.

After a forty-eight-mile trek north, Joseph arrives in the area he expects to find his brothers. He discovers they have departed. A man tells Joseph they have traveled fifteen miles further north to Dothan (Genesis 37:17). After this brief pause, Joseph continues his trek north for an additional fifteen miles. He has now traveled sixty-three miles one way on a trip he expects to be 126 miles to satisfy his father's instruction.

I see in this pause a glimpse into the Messiah's life on earth. He completes his preaching and healing ministry. He then "pauses" in the Garden of Gethsemane (Matthew 26:36). He then goes the remaining distance to complete His Father's will. (Luke 22:42; John 19:17).

Now see the potential consequence of favoritism in a family (Genesis 37:18). Joseph's brothers conspire to kill him before they even know why he has walked more than sixty miles to find them. For all they know, he might be about to announce the death of their father. That hadn't happened, but they didn't know that. The one thing they know for certain is that they want Joseph dead! They even plan a lie to tell their father (Genesis 37:20).

Reuben, Jacob's firstborn (Genesis 29:32, 35:23), was in charge. If anything bad happened to Joseph, it would be Reuben's fault. We should take our responsibilities in our families seriously. We should recognize error in our younger siblings and correct it by our words and actions. Reuben's counterplot appears to be in concert with his younger brother's plans. But his true motive is to save Joseph's life and prevent his brothers from committing a horrible sin. Reuben planned to deliver Joseph back to his father safely (Genesis 37:22).

Joseph's brothers must have been grazing the flock on high ground which allowed them to see Joseph approaching. The brother's plan to kill Joseph and Reuben's counterplan to rescue him took considerable time to formulate. They were watching Joseph approach. How did they know it was Joseph? There was only one coat like that in all of Canaan! The coat itself infuriated Joseph's brothers. It was a reminder of their own ill favor in the eyes of their father. It was a reminder of Joseph's dream of one day ruling over his family.

We are such pathetic creatures! The objects of our hatred are often inanimate. Joseph's brothers can't stand the sight of that coat another second. When he arrives, they are going to tear it off him.

Let's get inside Joseph's head for a minute. He sees the destination of his search for thirty minutes perhaps. He knows it's his brothers before they recognize him. He is so excited! He hasn't seen them for days. Now he found them! He's tired. He has walked sixty-three miles. He covers this last distance at a quicker pace. He can't wait to talk to them.

He arrives. What's the matter? They look angry. Before he can get "Shalom!" out of his mouth, he's on his back with his brothers on top of him! If any words are spoken by his brothers, they are words of hatred. The Bible doesn't record them. Violence against Joseph is planned. If Joseph speaks any words, they are words of pleading. Only Reuben listens. Reuben suggests casting Joseph into a nearby pit alive so he can rid him out of his brothers' hands later. Before the brothers did so, they striped Joseph out of his beautiful coat (Genesis 37:23–24, Mark 15:20).

Joseph is in the pit. He has been roughed up. He has no coat. And his brothers sit down to eat! (Genesis 37:25). Merchants were traveling from the east toward the southwest on their way to Egypt. It is interesting that Judah, Leah's fourth son, speaks up about profit. "What profit is it if we slay our brother and conceal his blood?" (Genesis 37:26). Judah, the head of the tribe from which the Messiah would eventually come, had an earthly profit in mind for himself. But the sparing of Joseph's life was to result in a spiritual profit that was intended by God for the benefit of the whole world. The brothers evidently agreed with the plan, and Joseph is sold for the price of a slave.

I have often wondered where Reuben was during this selling of Joseph. He knew his brothers wanted to kill Joseph. How could he have left them alone with Joseph? Judah had no right to speak or lead his brothers. Perhaps Reuben is tending the flock alone while his brothers eat.

I was an officer in the marine corps. The marine corps taught me many things about leadership. Don't order men to do what you wouldn't do. Lead by example. But at the same time, do not try to do everything yourself. Become comfortable ordering others. And whatever you do as an officer, do not endanger your own life simply because you don't want to endanger your men. Another principle that is often learned the hard way is learn how to recognize threats to your mission and prioritize them appropriately. Reuben forgot that one. Escaping livestock was not the greatest threat to his mission. As the oldest, Reuben was not only in charge of sheep. He was in charge of his brothers. And he knew they were the greatest threat to his mission. After learning of their plan to kill Joseph, how could he have left his brothers alone with Joseph for even a minute? But he did. Reuben was a poor leader and a bad example. That is not merely this author's assessment, it is God's. Reuben was unstable and untrustworthy (Genesis 35:22, 49:3–4). He shows poor judgement here once again. His brothers neither respect him nor listen to him. They operate totally outside his leadership, whether behind his back or to his face.

There may be another reason for this apparent shift in authority. Joseph is betrayed and sold for the price of a slave by someone you wouldn't suspect. A man close to him. A man named Judah. Christ was betrayed and sold for the price of a slave by someone you wouldn't suspect. A man close to him. A man named Judas. That is not too much of a stretch. If that isn't Old Testament typology, what is?

Joseph had to go to Egypt to keep those who wanted to kill him from being successful (Genesis 37:28). Does that sound at all familiar? Try reading (Matthew 2:13). "And when they were departed, behold, the angel of the Lord appeareth to Joseph in a dream, saying, Arise, and take the young child and his mother, and flee into Egypt, and be thou there until I bring thee word: for Herod will seek the young child to destroy him." What a coincidence!

Joseph had "died" although symbolically. He was going to be "dead" to his father. He was placed in a hewn pit. Next, he was "resurrected" from the pit. Does this sound familiar? It is one of those Old Testament glimpses into the future earthly life of the Messiah.

Poor Reuben returns. Nobody will listen to him. Note that he doesn't ask, "What are we going to do?" And he doesn't seem curious about what might happen to Joseph. No. He actually verbalizes his innermost feelings, "And I, wither shall I go?" (Genesis 37:29–30). Poor Reuben. Poor baby. It makes me want to slap him! Sorry, that's the marine in me coming out. Maybe it's the Holy Spirit, come to think of it. But I'd have slapped him!

Joseph's vesture is dipped in blood by friends from his own house (Genesis 37:31). He is wounded by people from his own house he thought were his friends. These same things would happen to Jesus. "And one shall say unto him, what are these wounds in thy hands? Then he shall answer, those with which I was wounded in the house of my friends" (Zechariah 13:6). "And he was clothed with a vesture dipped in blood: and his name is called The Word of God" (Revelation 19:13).

The lie is told (Genesis 37:32). The liar is lied to. Jacob had lied to his father when asked to say his name. Now his sons lie to him when he asks, "Where is Joseph?" We know what Reuben is thinking, *I wish I wasn't here. Dad thinks I've failed him again.* What about the other nine brothers? Remember, Benjamin, the youngest, wasn't in on the lie. He was another of Dad's favorites who had stayed at home. But I wonder what the other brothers thought. Were they equally culpable? If you know a lie and don't reveal it, do you "get points" for loyalty to the liar that cancel out your loss of points for not revealing the truth to the person to whom the lie was told? Before you waste too much time contemplating that one, I'll tell you the answer. No!

James 4:17 says, "Therefore to him that knoweth to do good and he doeth it not, to him it is sin." And Colossians 3:9 says, "Lie not one to another."

Picture the ultimate hypocrisy of Jacob's sons trying to cheer him up. It makes me want to slap their tearless faces! They deserve much worse. And was any of the money they'd received left? Had they already spent it? Did each brother take two pieces of silver? Did any change jingle in their pockets when they hugged their father? Had it all been spent? On what? What could you possibly find comfort in owning with money you received for selling your sibling as a slave? Could you buy something that would last? How I wonder what they purchased and what they thought about what was purchased.

The Ishmaelite merchants from Gilead sold Joseph for a lot more than twenty pieces of silver. Of that you can be certain. Potiphar, the captain of Pharaoh's palace police, purchased Joseph as a slave. Potiphar was a wealthy man.

Chapter 3

No, that isn't a misprint. I am asking a favor from you, the reader. I ask that you indulge me here. Read this book through to its end from here. Read chapter 2 in the order in which I have placed it. Although the reason for this request will become apparent later, I will offer a brief explanation here I hope will satisfy the most curious among you.

For many years of my Christian life, the story of Joseph was told to me by those who thought they knew it. All of them excluded the thirty-eighth chapter of Genesis. Chapter 38 seems on its surface to have absolutely nothing to do with what is happening to Joseph in Egypt. Why the Bible itself seems to do the same thing.

Read Genesis 37:36, "And the Midianites sold him [Joseph] into Egypt unto Potiphar, an officer of Pharaoh's, and captain of the guard." Now read Genesis 39:1, "And Joseph was brought down to Egypt; and Potiphar, an officer of Pharaoh, captain of the guard, an Egyptian, bought him at the hands of the Ishmeelites, which had brought him hither."

We don't learn anything new. We already knew Ishmaelites and Midianites are the same group in this story. We also didn't "learn" Potiphar was an Egyptian unless we might have thought he wasn't. I can't imagine why anyone would have suspected he might not be. It looks for now that chapter 38 can be left unread, and that no damage will be done to our story. So that is what we will do.

I just want to say, "Shame on those of you who put this book down and ran to the Bible and read Genesis chapter 38!" I'm joking of course. I could never find fault with anyone who puts down my words to read the Bible.

The first thing we are told in chapter 39 is the last thing any of us would have thought! "And the Lord was with Joseph" (Genesis 39:2a).

Excuse me? Joseph is in exactly the same position I find myself repeatedly in life! He is oppressed, lonely, suffering, forgotten, ill-treated, without hope, and forsaken by God! Well, isn't he? Don't tell me what you think you know because you've read the end of the story. Tell me what you'd think if this had happened to you and the story stopped here. That's where we always are when we experience life's troubles. We believe we know the future and are at an end.

I know there are Christians who possess great faith. I know there are Christians who trust God in all manner of circumstances. But sold as a slave by your siblings? Dead to your living parents? Working in a foreign country where you are not bilingual? I don't think many of us would recognize God at work right then.

"And the Lord was with Joseph; and he was a prosperous man" (Genesis 39:2a).

Be careful not to picture Joseph frolicking with the Lord and laughing. Be careful not to imagine him happy. In fact, the Bible tells us only that the Lord was with Joseph. It does not tell us that Joseph either knew it or felt it. It does not say that Joseph's newly gained prosperity brought him peace. My life experience has taught me prosperity often does the opposite. The more prosperity a man has, the greater are his problems.

I read in Hebrews 13:5 that the Lord will never leave me nor forsake me. I know that because it is inspired scripture, but I surely don't act as though I believe it sometimes. Jesus is our example in all things. Well, except sin. But you know what I mean. I don't follow His example consistently in many areas. In one, however, I do. In Mark 15:34, Jesus himself asked God the Father why He was forsaken. The fact that the Bible tells us that the Lord was with Joseph is no confirmation that Joseph thought so.

(Genesis 39:3–6) This is a little different. Joseph's Egyptian ruler saw something different about Joseph. He saw that the Lord was with him. What? Yes, he saw that it was the Lord who caused all Joseph did to prosper. This guy is an Egyptian! A godless Egyptian.

He doesn't know God. He probably had never heard of God before meeting Joseph. I don't know if Joseph was giving God credit for good things happening in his life, but Potiphar did. Isn't it amazing how even worldly people can recognize God's presence in our lives more readily than we can?

I once counselled a subordinate employee who was in a crisis in life. This person was in such a tailspin there was little hope of a good outcome. I remember thinking, *This guy is going to commit suicide! He has already decided.* I thought our meeting had been a total waste of time. I shared what I thought might be appropriate parts of God's word. I prayed. I left the person to continue his downward spiral. That was several years ago. Recently I received a letter from him. He wrote, "I could see God in your life, and I knew He would be there for me if I'd simply trust Him. I just didn't truly believe that the day we spoke." Later in the letter he wrote, "Thank you for saving my life that day!" That person's life is changed. It had nothing to do with my weak faith. It couldn't have. God had to accomplish something through me. God did that through Joseph to reach Potiphar with a truth. I'm not saying Potiphar was a believer. But what he saw in Joseph, God had revealed to him.

Potiphar makes Joseph the overseer of his household. Potiphar puts Joseph in such control that Potiphar loses track of all he owns! He is only certain about what he has on his plate (Genesis 39:4–6). Joseph is "well favored." He's a foreign teenager!

(Genesis 39:7–20) Are you kidding me? This just insists on going from great to terrible every time! Have you ever been sold as a slave by your family? Me either. What was my big problem again? I'm embarrassed to tell anyone. And now Joseph is about to inherit a problem that will make being sold as a slave by his brothers seem like a vacation!

Potiphar is a busy man. Or maybe Joseph is doing such a great job taking care of Potiphar's affairs that Potiphar has time to be out recreating somewhere. Of one thing we can be certain. Potiphar's wife needs more to do. She has time to lie around the house and seduce teenagers. And she casts her eyes upon Joseph. She says, "Lie with me!"

Well, any first-time reader of the Bible knows how this is going to turn out. A lonely young man with raging hormones, a brother hated by his brothers, a son who is dead to his father, a kid in a foreign country who doesn't understand their customs, a teenager in charge of a big house with a beautiful (you know she was) wicked woman begging for sex…let's see…I'd gladly have given anyone hundred to one odds he'd be in bed with her in ten minutes…five minutes!

Look at verse eight. Is this boy normal? The answer dear reader is no! Maybe you finally get it. Joseph is an Old Testament type of Christ! It just wouldn't have worked if he had done, what I'm afraid…no…certain, the majority of seventeen-year-old young men would have done!

This doesn't happen just once. Joseph refuses her daily. How many days? The Bible doesn't say, but I'll bet it was lots. Joseph speaks to her about his responsibilities as a worker. He speaks of his loyalty to Potiphar. But look at the end of verse 9, "How can I do this great wickedness and sin against God?" I'll tell you, Joseph. God forsook you, so who cares? I mean it's all right to be obedient to God if He blesses you and makes your life a joy. I'd understand that. But to care about your sins after God allowed your brothers to sell you as a slave? At the age of seventeen? I don't think so! But notice that Joseph doesn't say, "How could someone…" or "How could a person…," he makes it personal. "How then can I do this great wickedness and sin against God?"

Joseph has things to do that require his presence in the house. One day, he goes into the house alone. Potiphar's wife is close by. Verse 11 describes the scene. She is close. Close enough to catch his garment. "Lie with me" (Verse 12). She demands for the umpteenth time.

Joseph flees leaving his garment in her grip.

I don't know if he ran out naked or if anyone had seen the incident, but it didn't make any difference. Potiphar's wife knew what she desired was never going to happen. Joseph was never going to lie with her. She had been scorned by a Hebrew teen. She'd show him! She screams!

Think of the hypocrisy and level of sin in this woman. She who coveted, she who begged for adultery, she it is who cries out. She has been insulted. She has been ill-treated. She has been mocked. She has been attacked. She was nearly raped on her own bed by this Hebrew boy that "he" (Potiphar) stupidly brought into their house. She's going to stay pretty close to that garment because it's her only evidence. Potiphar returns and hears the story. Of course he believes his wife. Even if he doesn't, he is forced to act as if he does.

Joseph is falsely accused and taken into custody. Sound familiar? Matthew 26:60.

"But the Lord was with Joseph" (Genesis 39:21). Give me a break! Never in the history of man to this point was there a human being who epitomized a person forsaken by God more than Joseph! He's done nothing wrong really. Oh, he's a sinner all right, but the Bible doesn't record any. But he's at the bottom now! Why? Don't miss this! Because he is now precisely where God needs him to be to accomplish God's will on earth.

You see, here's the mistake we make. We wrongly assume we have to be problem free and at the pinnacle of life to be effectively used by God. But look around you. The family of God is inhabited by quadriplegic artists, motivational speakers with MS, legless war survivors tramping for Christ, and other Christians from diverse backgrounds whose lives and testimonies are walking paradoxes!

The apostle Paul testifies in 2 Corinthians 12:10, "Therefore I take pleasure in infirmities, in reproaches, in necessities, in persecutions, in distress for Christ's sake: for when I am weak, then am I strong." I certainly never learned *that* in the marine corps!

I don't know about you, but I'd prefer the Lord to show me mercy a different way. Yeah, I'll pass on the being sold as a slave to a foreigner by my family, being falsely accused of attempted rape by my master's wife, being thrown into prison without a trial, and then finding favor with the warden. Thanks anyway!

(Genesis 39:21–23) I give up! Joseph just must be stupid! This is exactly what happened last time! I can predict with 100 percent certainty that this is going to turn out badly. I learn from my lessons in life. When I'm trusting the Lord for protection in some area of my life and circumstances deteriorate, I avoid that area. I would never be so dumb as to think when things are going to crap (sorry) that "the

Lord was with Duke and shewed him mercy." Why if the Lord was doing all that, I wouldn't have any problems, would I? Well, would I? What do you think? Don't give the answer you think I want to hear. What do you really think? How do you react to adversity in life? I'll bet I know how you react. You think all your troubles come from Satan, don't you? Don't tell me. Tell God.

Listen, a teenage girl dove off a dock. Her head hit the bottom, and she broke her neck. The foolish among us ask, "Where was God?" I'll tell you where God was. The Lord was with Joni Erickson. That's where he was! And he showed her mercy. She didn't drown. And she doesn't even know me, but she has blessed my life profoundly with hope and rejoicing, and she has given me courage! I'm a former active duty marine. I flew helicopters in Vietnam. I got hit several times by enemy fire. But I get my strength from the Lord. Thanks to people like Joni! And someday in the kingdom, I'm going to run up to her—no—make that she's going to run up to me (she'll be able to run there) and throw her arms around me and just smile. Now she's going to be in charge of something pretty special in the kingdom. I won't be. She has yielded her life to the Lord. I want to keep mine most days. But Joni Erickson "gets it." She understands that the Lord was "with" Joseph in spite of how the circumstances of his life appear to us.

God needs former prostitutes, drug addicts, paraplegics, quadriplegics, blind, deaf, alcoholics, people from diverse sordid backgrounds to receive the gift of salvation. He can then use those people to reach others, some of whom are currently going through those same kinds of struggles.

It wouldn't surprise me if Joseph were to meet a couple of prisoners going through the same anguish he was (Genesis 40:1–4). Bingo! Wow! That was fast! I wonder what a butler and a baker could have done to kindle the Pharaoh's ire enough to land them in the slammer. Notice that Joseph was "bound" there. So much for God showing him mercy huh? Well, he did win favor with the keeper of the prison. But don't forget, Joseph had also "won favor" with Potiphar. I'm a bit skeptical. Maybe the relationship with these two will work out better.

(Genesis 40:5–8) Uh-oh! Dreams! This doesn't sound good. Every one of Joseph's problems began with dreams, didn't they? Just keep your mouth shut and ignore them, Joseph. It's so easy for me to not share what I know about God with people! Remaining silent when I have lots to say is one of my greatest gifts! I find it much easier to talk to people about football, farming, food, fishing…you know, issues that are relatively meaningless in the grand scheme of things. Talking about meaningless stuff seldom offends anyone.

Joseph is so not like me. Maybe it's because he is so much like Christ! I don't like that thought very much. How could he blurt out that dream interpretations belong to God? And further, if he thinks they do belong to God, why does Joseph want to hear them? Aren't dreams from God responsible for his brothers hating him and for him being in prison now?

The chief butler speaks up. "In my dream, behold, a vine was before me; and in the vine were three branches: and it was as though it budded, and her blossoms shot forth; and the clusters thereof brought forth ripe grapes: and Pharaoh's cup was in my hand: and I took the grapes, and pressed them into Pharaoh's cup, and I gave the cup into Pharaoh's hand" (Genesis 40:9–11).

I'm going to ask you a question. Do you trust God? Every Christian reading this probably is thinking, "Sure!" But do you trust Him to come through for you when you really need Him? How about after your siblings sold you as a slave to foreigners, and you get falsely accused of a crime and thrown in prison? Right then, tell me you trust God to come through for you when you need Him. I know you don't! If the truth were known, you probably don't trust Him even though your life isn't going anywhere nearly as badly as Joseph's. We're all like that.

Here is a nugget for you. This is one of those pieces of advice that can change your weak faith into a strength. It's simple. You don't have to be smart to "get it." Read this story in the Bible that appears to be about Joseph and think about it. Think of how Joseph reacts to adversity in life. Think about how it would be quite reasonable and justifiable for him to react. Think of how you would have reacted. If there is a difference, what is God telling you about your faith? We read these stories in the Bible, and we act as if they are just words on a page. We think we are reading a history book at best. We forget that

God is speaking to us! He isn't simply telling a story. He isn't telling a story about Joseph. The entire Bible is about Jesus!

Joseph trusts God not based on the circumstances of his life but on the basis of the simple fact that God is God! Do you get that? I'm not sure you do. The sovereignty of God scares most of us a little. I think we "trust" God mostly when we are free of life's problems.

This story that appears to be about Joseph is an Old Testament type of Christ. You may begin to see that. But Joseph's story is more than that. It is an illustration God doesn't want you to miss. God wants you to trust Him in spite of the fact that you really fear He may have forsaken you. Never forget that the lousy circumstances of our lives may be part of a plan God has to accomplish something great. Now listen, Joseph is not suffering the consequences of his past sin. Joseph is where God needs him.

> And Joseph said unto him, "This is the interpretation of it: The three branches are three days: Yet within three days shall Pharaoh lift up thine head, and restore thee unto thy place: and thou shalt deliver Pharaoh's cup into his hand, after the former manner when thou wast his butler. But think on me when it shall be well with thee, and shew kindness, I pray thee, unto me, and make mention of me unto Pharaoh, and bring me out of this house: For indeed I was stolen away out of the land of the Hebrews: and here also have I done nothing that they should put me into the dungeon." (Genesis 40:12–15)

> When the chief baker saw that the interpretation was good, he said unto Joseph, "I also was in my dream, and, behold, I had white baskets on my head: And in the upper basket there was all manner of bakemeats for Pharaoh; and the birds did eat them out of the basket on my head. (Genesis 40:16–17)

Joseph tells the baker the three baskets are three days, and at the end of the three days, the baker will be beheaded, and birds will eat his flesh.

Three days go by, and everything comes to pass exactly as God had revealed it to Joseph. The baker is dead. The butler gets out of prison and is restored to his former position.

Now read Genesis 40:23. Let's talk about that. You, not Joseph, are in prison. A cellmate tells you a dream that's been bothering him. You tell him not to worry about a thing. In three days, he is not only going to be free, but he won't be doing time in a halfway house or even on parole! You tell the dreamer that he is going to be working at his former job for the guy who pressed charges and got him put in prison to begin with. Okay follow this with me. Don't just read it. Think about it. Do you think it remotely possible for your freed cellmate to forget about you? Of course you don't! Day one gets checked off. Day two. And on day three, your former cellmate gets done for him exactly what you had predicted! He'd be telling everybody about you! He'd be telling that story for the rest of his life!

The butler didn't simply forget about Joseph due to the excitement of the moment. No, he forgets about Joseph for two years. Now unless the butler was suffering from some sort of dementia, there is no earthly way he could have forgotten about Joseph. And there you have it! It simply wasn't time for Joseph to be released. Had Joseph been released at that time, there was nothing to keep him in Egypt. He would have walked back to Canaan. God had reached down and blotted any memory of Joseph from the butler's brain! God knew that Joseph had two more dreams to interpret.

Chapter 4

> And it came to pass at the end of two full years, that Pharaoh dreamed: and, behold, he stood by the river. And, behold, there came up out of the river seven well favored kine and fat fleshed; and they fed in a meadow. And, behold, seven other kine came up after them out of the river, ill favoured and leanfleshed; and stood by the other kine upon the brink of the river. And the ill favoured and leanfleshed kine did eat up the seven well favoured and fat kine, So Pharaoh awoke. And he slept and dreamed the second time: and, behold, seven ears of corn came up on one stalk, rank and good. And, behold, seven thin ears blasted with the east wind came up after them. And the seven thin ears devoured the seven rank and full ears. And pharaoh awoke, and, behold, it was a dream.
> —Genesis 41:1–8

Pharaoh is troubled. He calls for all of Egypt's top magicians. They hear the dreams. They're all stumped! They have no idea what the dreams mean. God intervenes. God causes the butler to remember Joseph after the butler had been brain-dead for two years. The butler tells Pharaoh about Joseph. Pharaoh says, "Go get him!"

Now Joseph has been in prison thirteen years! He hasn't shaved nor cut his hair. His clothes are rags. Joseph gets a haircut and shave and new clothes according to the Bible. I hope he also got a quick bath. And he finds himself standing in front of Pharaoh. Pharaoh is probably tired of telling people about his dreams, but he does so once more. He adds, "I have heard that you can interpret dreams." Look how Joseph humbly answers. "It is not in me: God shall give Pharaoh an answer of peace" (Genesis 41:16). How did Joseph know it would be an answer of peace? For all he knew, God might be going to destroy Egypt and Pharaoh with it!

Pharaoh tells Joseph the dreams. Joseph informs Pharaoh of seven years of plenty coming quickly which will be followed by seven years of famine. Then Joseph goes completely off the rails! He starts telling Pharaoh how to stay alive during the famine. Are you kidding me, Joseph? What if you're wrong? What if your ideas about food storage aren't quite as good as you think they are? Did Joseph think he knew how to do all that? No! Joseph knew that God knew how. Joseph wasn't worried. You and I would have been worried. Joseph wasn't. And just as God has placed what might seem like crazy ideas in the minds of men throughout the history of man (build a big boat, sling a rock at a giant, douse a pile of wood with water three times and then ask me to light it from heaven), he places these thoughts in Joseph's mind.

I have to laugh when I think about Joseph's personality. He dreams a dream where he's lord over his family, and he shares it. He listens to the dreams of two fellow inmates in prison and tells them their future. Pharaoh has a dream, and Joseph blurts out what it means. Now he's telling Pharaoh how to run Egypt for the next fourteen years! As far as Joseph knows, he's only two out of six on dream interpretations. Remember, his first two dreams about ruling over his brothers and parents haven't come to pass yet either.

If I had been in Joseph's place, things would have turned out differently. I can keep a secret forever! I can keep a secret till I forget about it! I wouldn't have told my family about my dreams. They would have had to hate me for some other reason. I don't like to think of how the Potiphar's wife incident might have turned out if it had been me at seventeen. I never would have let on to the butler and baker I perceived they were sad. I wouldn't have heard their dreams nor suspected that God would tell me what they meant. If I had been in prison for eleven years in a foreign country, I wouldn't have been talking to anyone. Think of yourself. Out of the three, who should have looked the saddest? The butler and baker who had been pondering confusing dreams for a few hours? Or might Joseph have looked just a little sadder after being in prison in a foreign country eleven years for something he didn't do? Talk to the butler and baker about why they looked so sad? Not likely! I certainly wouldn't have. I'm too self-oriented. Then when the butler got out, I wouldn't have been remembered by him…ever!

The body of Christ is made up of people with different gifts. God uses us all. Well, He can use us all if we let Him. I want you to get this…God has Joseph exactly where He needs him. Nothing has gone wrong in Joseph's life to this point. Something great is about to happen!

(Genesis 41:37–46) Having a bold witness allows the world to see God working in your life. Joseph boldly said, "God shall give Pharaoh an answer" (Genesis 41:16). He did not say what those of weaker faith may have said, something like, "Why don't you try to ask God what the dream means? I ask Him for stuff, and sometimes it works. But I've been praying to get out of prison for thirteen years, and it hasn't worked yet." No, Joseph speaks boldly. God's power doesn't depend on the circumstances of Joseph's life.

> And Joseph said unto Pharaoh, The dream of Pharaoh is one: God hath shewed Pharaoh what he is about to do. The seven good kine are seven years; the seven good ears are seven years: the dream is one. And the seven thin and ill favoured kine that came up after them are seven years; and the seven empty ears blasted with the east wind shall be seven years of famine. This is the thing which I have spoken unto Pharaoh: What God is about to do he sheweth unto Pharaoh. Behold there come seven years of plenty throughout all the land of Egypt: and there shall arise after them seven years of famine; and all the plenty shall be forgotten in the land of Egypt; and the famine

shall consume the land; and the plenty shall not be known in the land by reason of the famine following; for it shall be very grievous. And for the dream was doubled unto Pharaoh twice: it is because the thing is established by God, and God will shortly bring it to pass. Now therefore let Pharaoh look out a man discreet and wise, and set him over the land of Egypt. Let Pharaoh do this, and let him appoint officers over the land, and take up the fifth part of the land of Egypt in the seven plenteous years. And let them gather all the food of those good years that come, and lay up corn under the hand of Pharaoh, and let them keep food in the cities. And that food shall be for store to the land against the seven years of famine, which shall be in the land of Egypt; that the land perish not through the famine. (Genesis 41:25–36)

Pharaoh thinks Joseph's idea is a good one. So do his servants of course. And Pharaoh can tell the Spirit of God is in Joseph. Could someone tell the Spirit of God is in you? Or would they say, "He is? Could have fooled me!" Pharaoh goes on to say he understands that God is the one who has shown Joseph all this. Then he places Joseph in charge of Egypt—not just "king for a day" but for fourteen years! Pharaoh takes off his ring, the ring that let's everyone know he is Pharaoh, and places it on Joseph. Pharaoh arrays Joseph in beautiful clothes and places a gold chain around his neck. He places Joseph in a chariot, and servants cry out before him, "Bow the knee!" And Pharaoh makes Joseph ruler over all the land of Egypt. And he informs Joseph, "No man shall lift up his hand or foot in all of Egypt without your approval!" Oh, and Pharaoh gives Joseph a new name, Zaphnath-Paaneah. He also gave Joseph a wife.

Joseph is thirty years old (Genesis 41:46). He had been sold as a slave thirteen years ago. He is now ready to start the "ministry" God has for him on this earth. His age is no coincidence. "And Jesus himself began to be about 30 years of age" (Luke 3:23). Jesus was thirty when He started His earthly ministry. What is Joseph's real connection to Christ? We see many ways he is an Old Testament "type" of Christ. But is there some other connection? Does it have anything to do with what is happening outside of Egypt? Let's go on.

Now Joseph goes "out from the presence of Pharaoh, and throughout all the land of Egypt." I'll tell you the first place I would have gone. I'd have arrested Potiphar's wife and put her in prison. Then I would have found Pharaoh's butler who left me in prison for two more years and maybe done the same to him. But those are the kinds of things we do when we get to thinking, "Life's all about me!" And it clearly is not.

Chapter 5

> Now when Jacob saw that there was corn in Egypt, Jacob said to his sons, why do ye look one upon another? And he said, Behold, I have heard there is corn in Egypt: get you down thither, and buy for us from thence; that we may live and not die. And Joseph's ten brethren went down to buy corn in Egypt. But Benjamin, Joseph's brother, Jacob sent not with his brethren: for he said, Lest peradventure mischief befall him. (Gen. 42: 1–4)

Joseph's father, Jacob, is with his other sons and their families back in what would one day be called Israel. The famine was grievous there as well, and life had been difficult for two years. Jacob had heard, no doubt from travelling merchants, of food being available in Egypt. He tells his sons to stop standing around, looking at each other, and get down to Egypt to purchase bread and avoid death by starvation. The ten oldest sons go, but once again, Jacob has a favorite, Benjamin.

Movies I've seen portraying this story have always depicted Benjamin as a young boy. He wasn't. He was no lad in the sense we use the term today. He was about thirty-five. He may have looked young, but he was married and had ten sons (Gen. 46:21). Benjamin was a man quite capable of making the trip to Egypt with his brothers. His father (Jacob) was doing the same thing with him that he had done with Joseph. I can only imagine Benjamin's brothers were jealous of him and resented his special treatment.

> And the sons of Israel came to buy corn among those that came: for the famine was in the land of Canaan. (Gen. 42:5)

Joseph is now thirty-seven years old. He had ten older brothers, so Ruben is near fifty. These ten men have been together all their lives. I doubt they'd ever left Canaan before. The sixty-three-mile grazing trip they had taken to Dothan was probably as far as they had travelled from home I'd guess. Now they travel south and west across the northern Sinai peninsula roughly 230 miles to Egypt, the country into which they had sold their brother. Do you think they thought about it along the way? Did any one of them dare to bring it up? Do you think they thought of Joseph having travelled this same way bound? Don't you wonder whether they thought he might be living? Wouldn't you have thought of your sibling every day of your life? Wouldn't you have loathed yourself? What a horrible, quiet, hungry, wordless trip this must have been! How frightened they were. Would they be suspected of having money with them and be robbed along the way? Might they be killed? Would they ever reach home with the food they hoped to purchase? This was no vacation. This was one scary trip!

> And Joseph was governor over the land, and he it was that sold to all the people of the land: and Joseph's brethren came, and bowed down themselves before him with their faces to the earth. (Gen. 42:6)

How things have changed for Joseph! He has progressed from a bound slave and prisoner to "ruler of Egypt." He is governor of the land. He is revered by all people from the lowliest slave to Pharaoh himself! He has become a hero of Egypt! His wisdom came from God, and even Pharaoh acknowledges that! Unfortunately for Pharaoh, admitting God is with someone doesn't make one a believer. But Joseph is a believer as we shall see!

Joseph's brothers arrive. Had Joseph expected them? Had he hoped for them? His brothers avoid eye contact with this important Egyptian ruler. This Zaphnathpaaneah is one scary dude! You know they had to be thinking they'd rather have starved to death back home than to have been here!

Joseph was thinking something far different. He recognizes them. He remembered his dream about sheaves, "We were binding sheaves in the field, and lo, my sheaf arose, and also stood upright, and behold, your sheaves stood round about, and made obeisance to my sheaf." And it had now come true!

> And Joseph saw his brethren, and he knew them, but made himself strange to them, and spake roughly to them; and he said to them, Whence come ye? And they said, from the land of Canaan to buy food. And Joseph knew his brethren, but they knew not him. And Joseph remembered the dreams which he dreamed of them, and he said unto them, Ye are spies; to see the nakedness of the land are ye come. And they said to him, Nay my lord, but to buy food are thy servants come. We are one man's sons; we are true men, thy servants are no spies. And he said unto them, Nay, but to see the nakedness of the land ye are come. And they said, Thy servants are twelve brethren, the sons of one man in the land of Canaan; and, behold, the youngest is this day with our father, and one is not. And Joseph said unto them, that is it that I spake unto you, saying, Ye are spies: Hereby ye shall be proved: By the life of Pharaoh ye shall not go forth hence except your youngest brother come hither. Send one of you, and let him fetch your brother, and ye shall be kept in prison, that your words may be proved whether

> there be any truth in you: or else by the life of
> Pharaoh surely ye are spies. And he put them all
> together into ward three days. (Gen. 42: 7–17)

Joseph knows they speak the truth. They even made a minor reference to Joseph's former existence, "And one is not." But Joseph must make certain he doesn't lose contact with them. He can do anything he pleases. He's "ruler of Egypt!" He informs them that nine of them are required to stay in Egypt as prisoners while one brother returns to Canaan to fetch Benjamin and return with him. Then he places all ten of them in prison for three days. Three days! He was in prison for thirteen years!

> And Joseph said unto them the third day, This
> do and live; for I fear God: If ye be true men,
> let one of your brethren be bound in the house
> of your prison: go ye, carry corn for the famine
> of your houses: But bring your youngest brother
> unto me; so shall your words be verified, and ye
> shall not die. And they did so. (Gen. 42:18–20)

Joseph is speaking Egyptian. His brothers don't know what he's saying until the interpreter speaks to them in Hebrew. I'll bet as they looked at the interpreter their heads snapped to look at Joseph when they heard he feared their God. They at least stared at the floor, and their eyes got big.

Zaphnathpaaneah had spoken. There was no further discussion. The Egyptians and the brothers had to do what he said. They were all thinking there was no way their father would ever allow Benjamin, his new favorite son, to travel to Egypt. He was the only son remaining (or so Jacob thought) that was born to Joseph's mother, Rachel. He had loved Rachel so. She had died during childbirth during the birth of Benjamin (Gen. 35:16–20).

> And they said one to another, we are verily guilty
> concerning our brother, in that we saw the anguish

> of his soul, when he besought us, and we would not hear; therefore is this distress come upon us. And Ruben answered them, saying, Spake I not unto you, saying, Do not sin against the child; and ye would not hear? therefore, behold, also his blood is required. And they knew not that Joseph understood them; for he spake to them by an interpreter. (Gen. 42:21–24)

Joseph listens to his brothers openly discuss their treatment of him twenty years ago. They speak in Hebrew of course, thinking, *This Egyptian doesn't understand what we're talking about.* Weak leader, Ruben, whines something like, "I told you so." I picture him grimacing and stomping his foot as he speaks. As always, his brothers ignore him. If he had done his job, if he had demanded his brothers release Joseph, if he had fought them, and if he had stayed near Joseph while Joseph was in the pit, he may have prevented all this. He'd have been a better leader, but that was not God's plan. Joseph can't bear to listen, and he leaves.

Joseph gathers his composure and returns. He takes Simeon and places him in chains before their eyes. Joseph might like the thought of Ruben having to explain all this to his father when he returns to Canaan with the food. It also would have been difficult for one brother to make it back home with all the food and animals while the rest remained in prison in Egypt. Simeon was the next oldest, most likely in his late forties. Simeon is fairly certain his father will never allow Benjamin go to Egypt, so he's thinking he may be in prison for life, never to see his family again. Simeon had six sons, perhaps some daughters, and a Canaanite wife.

> Then Joseph commanded their sacks to be filled with corn, and to restore every man's money into his sack, and to give them provision for the way: and thus did he unto them. And they laded their asses with corn, and departed thence. And as one of them opened his sack to give his ass provender

> in the inn, he espied his money; for behold, it was in his sack's mouth. And he said unto his brethren, My money is restored; and, lo, it is even in my sack: and their heart failed them, and they were afraid, saying one to another, What is this that God hath done unto us? (Gen. 42:25–28)

Joseph had done all this of course. Nothing in Egypt was done without Joseph having given the order. He had even provided food for them on their trip. You know it was great food! Joseph was doing what Jesus has told us to do.

> But I say unto you. Love your enemies, bless them that curse you, and pray for them which despitefully use you, and persecute you. (Matt. 5:44)

You say, "Come on now! Joseph was playing a mean trick on his brothers!" Was that his motive here? Really? Is what he did anything like what you would have done? Yeah, you would have made sure the food they had been given for their trip was the best in Egypt. That's what you would have done. Sure it is. I think you would have made your mean brothers pay! I would have.

Can you imagine the absolute horror of finding your money in your sack? Rather, Zaphnathpaaneah's money? I really think Joseph simply wanted to give them free grain. He never takes them to task over it. But that had to be a fright for them. Did we forget to pay? Will they think we stole it? What a nightmare! "What is this that God hath done unto us?" So you think God has been angry with you boys for these twenty years? What wretched lives!

Chapter 6

And they came to Jacob their father unto the land of Canaan, and told him all that befell unto them; saying, the man, who is the lord of the land, spake roughly to us, and took us for spies of the country. And we said unto him, We are true men; we are no spies: We be twelve brethren, sons of our father; one is not, and the youngest is this day with our father in the land of Canaan. And the man, the Lord of the country, said unto us, Hereby shall I know that ye are true men; leave one of your brethren here with me, and take for the famine of your households, and be gone: And bring your youngest brother to me: then shall I know that ye are no spies, but that ye are true men: so will I deliver you your brother, and ye shall traffick in the land. And it came to pass as they emptied their sacks, that, behold, every man's money was in his sack: and when both they and their father saw the bundles of money, they were afraid. And Jacob their father said unto them, Me have ye bereaved of my children: Joseph is not, and Simeon is not, and ye will take Benjamin away: all these things are against me. (Gen. 42: 29–36)

Usually, it's good to get home after a long trip. You know, like a 230-mile trip walking next to a donkey. Not this time. They tell Jacob about Benjamin having to go to Egypt with them when they return for more food should that become necessary. Simeon will be in prison for life if they don't go back. This isn't one of Jacob's better days. Now, there's the money problem due to the fact they didn't pay for what they bought. At least that's what they think.

Poor Jacob is beside himself! Instead of rejoicing over food during the famine, he has lost another son and is certain he'll lose a third should Benjamin be taken to Egypt. He feels as if his sons are ganging up on him. Perhaps worse, that God has forsaken him.

But wait! Perhaps there is a solution! Ruben has a plan! He has given this a lot of thought. He approaches his father. "Dad...I've got it!" (Gen. 42:37). "...Slay my two sons, if I bring him (Benjamin) not to thee: deliver him into my hand, and I will bring him to thee again." What kind of senseless drivel is this? The way Jacob is supposed to get over the loss of his favorite son is to kill two of his grandchildren! What on earth is Ruben smoking? How can he even get those words out? And why not just suggest killing you, Ruben? That would make a lot more sense! I'll tell you what, Jacob needs some advice on parenting. Ruben *never* would have been in charge of so much as a three-legged dog that belonged to me after this outburst! I'd have lined up all my sons and said, "Ruben is relieved of command. Judah is in charge. Ruben is now last among you. Dismissed." Sorry, that's the marine in me.

Jacob doesn't give Ruben's suggestion much thought (Gen. 42:38). Immediately, Jacob says, "My son shall not go down with you, for his brother (Joseph) is dead, and he (Benjamin) is left alone: if mischief befall him by the way in which ye go, then ye shall bring down my gray hairs with sorrow to the grave." Guess he didn't like the idea of killing two of his grandchildren after learning he'd never see Benjamin again. Do you have any grandchildren? I'm a grandfather of eleven, six boys and five girls. Not wanting to risk the life of one of his grandchildren or killing two of his grandchildren certainly seems reasonable to me. But don't miss this. Jacob, in trying to keep Benjamin safe, was working against God's plan. What seemed to him to be reasonable to do was potentially preventing God's will.

In Isaiah 43:2, we learn something a little scary. God says, "When thou walkest through the fire, thou shalt not be burned."

God doesn't say, "Don't worry, you'll never have to walk through fire." I had to smile when I first read that. I had to walk through fire after a helicopter crash in Vietnam. I believe God was with me. The point is, God brings about His will in many different ways. Some of those ways aren't what we would choose. That is precisely where Jacob finds himself now. Benjamin isn't going to Egypt, and that's final.

> And the famine was sore in the land. And it came to pass when they had eaten up the corn which they had brought out of Egypt, their father said unto them, Go again, buy us a little food. And Judah spake unto him, saying, The man did solemnly protest unto us, saying, Ye shall not see my face, except your brother be with you. If thou wilt send our brother with us, we will go down and buy thee food: But if thou wilt not send him, we will not go down: for the man said unto us, Ye shall not see my face, except your brother be with you. And Israel said, wherefore dealt ye so ill with me, as to tell the man whether ye had yet a brother? And they said, The man asked us straitly of our state, and of our kindred, saying, Is your father yet alive? have ye another brother? and we told him after the tenor of these words: could we certainly know that he would say, Bring your brother down? And Judah said to Israel his father, Send the lad with me, and we will arise and go; that we may live, and not die, both we and also our little ones. I will be surety for him; of my hand shalt thou require him; if I bring him not unto thee, and set him before thee, then let me bare the blame forever: For except we had lingered, surely now we had returned this second time. (Gen. 43:1–10)

Jacob is getting old. He forgets things. After all, he's 130 (Gen. 47:28)! Judah speaks softly to his father. Maybe Jacob had done what I suggested and made Judah the leader, but the Bible doesn't record it. But Ruben doesn't speak. Simeon is in prison in Egypt. I don't know where Levi is. Those three are older than Judah. But Simeon and Levi had murdered a whole city of innocent men (Gen. 34:25). So maybe they weren't fit for command either. Judah speaks sensibly, "Send Benjamin with me that we may all live. I will be surety for him." Jacob gives his approval.

> And their father Israel said unto them, If it must be so now, do this; take of the best fruits in the land in your vessels, and carry down the man a present, a little balm, and a little honey, spices, and myrrh, nuts, and almonds: And take double money in your hand; and the money that was brought again in the mouth of your sacks, carry it again in your hand; peradventure it was an oversight: Take also your brother, and arise, go again unto the man: And God Almighty give you mercy before the man, that he may send away your other brother, and Benjamin. If I be bereaved of my children, I am bereaved. (Gen. 43:11–14).

So Jacob truly relents! Okay, but doesn't the plan make you smile a little? Listen to how frightened he is. Take lots of stuff, our nicest stuff, stuff that's even too nice for us to use except on special occasions. Also, take double money, plus the money you all found in your sacks. Triple money! And take my most precious thing, take Benjamin. (Don't forget, Benjamin is about thirty-five years old). And Jacob continues by saying he hopes God will get them home, but he has zero confidence he'll see any of them again. And he'll miss Benjamin more than any of them.

> And the men took that present, and they took double money in their hand, and Benjamin; and rose up, and went down to Egypt, and stood before Joseph. (Gen. 43:15)

Off go eleven brothers to Egypt. Judah is in charge. Judah is responsible for the success of the mission. He is responsible for Benjamin's safety. Ruben's last recorded words in the Bible were the ridiculous suggestion that Jacob might be interested in killing two of his grandchildren. That was "big" of Ruben, don't you think? He makes a mistake and his children get to pay for it with their lives. "Thanks, Dad!" If Ruben says anything else in his life, God didn't think it was important enough to record in the Bible.

The eleven brothers arrive in Egypt. They have travelled on donkeys roughly 240 miles one way. I own two donkeys, Obadiah (Obi) and Micah. I bought Obi first following the advice of an old farmer I knew. There were two pit bulls that would pester my goats and cows in a couple of pastures on my farm. My friend said to me, "Duke, you need a watch donkey." He said with a donkey in the pasture, I wouldn't need to worry about the pit bulls, coyotes, or anything else bothering my livestock. I had very little faith a donkey could do much about the dogs, but I bought Obi and put him in one pasture with my goats. Not too long after, the pit bulls made a visit to what they thought was a goat pasture. The problem was, it had become a goat/donkey pasture. I happened to be nearby. Wow! My friend was an experienced farmer, and I started following more of his advice after that. Oh, the dogs haven't been back. It wasn't pretty, but it was fun to watch.

The whole reason for bringing up Obi was to talk about his speed while doing work. He doesn't have any. He can do a lot of things. He can drag logs, pull stumps, drag deer out of the woods, pull carts, but everything he does, including coming to food when he's hungry, he does at one speed. Slow! I can't imagine following

Obi 240 miles. Trust me, this wasn't a fun trip, and it took almost two weeks. What the brothers were thinking made the trip seem even longer.

> And when Joseph saw Benjamin with them, he said to the ruler of his house, Bring these men home, and slay, and make ready; for these men shall dine with me at noon. And the man did as Joseph bade; and the man brought the men into Joseph's house. And the men were afraid, because they were brought into Joseph's house; and they said, because of the money that was returned in our sacks at the first time are we brought in; that he may seek occasion against us, and fall upon us, and take us for bondmen, and our asses. And they came near to the steward of Joseph's house, and they communed with him at the door of the house, and said, O sir, we came indeed down at the first time to buy food: And it came to pass, when we came to the inn, that we opened our sacks, and behold, every man's money was in the mouth of his sack, our money in full weight: and we have brought it again in our hand. And other money have we brought down in our hands to buy food: we cannot tell who put our money in our sacks. And he said, Peace be to you, fear not; your God, and the God of your father, hath given you treasure in your sacks: I had your money. And he brought Simeon out unto them. (Gen. 43:16–23)

The brothers are now standing before Joseph. If Simeon can see through the bars, you know he has to be straining his neck to see whether Benjamin is with them. Joseph sees Benjamin. And he instructs his servants (in Egyptian) to make a feast. He has his brothers taken to his house. They don't have any idea what is being said or where they are being taken. *Why are we being taken to Zaphnathpaaneah's house?* they must wonder. *He's either going to make us slaves, or he's going to kill us! they're thinking.* They apologize to the steward for not having paid last time. Look what he says! "Your God and the God of your father has given you treasure in your sacks. I have your money." They have to be thinking, *How can this Egyptian know anything about God? And how can he speak Hebrew?* They don't expect lunch. They expect death or slavery.

> And the man brought the men into Joseph's house, and gave them water, and they washed their feet; and he gave their asses provender. And they made ready the present against Joseph came at noon: for they heard that they should eat bread there. And when Joseph came home, they brought him the present which was in their hand into the house, and bowed themselves to him to the earth. And he asked them of their welfare, and said, Is your father well, the old man of whom ye spake? Is he yet alive? And they answered, Thy servant our father is in good health, he is yet alive. And they bowed their heads, and made obeisance. And he lifted up his eyes, and saw his brother Benjamin, his mother's son, and said, Is this your younger brother, of whom ye spake unto me? And he said, God be gracious unto thee, my son. And Joseph made haste; for his bowels did yearn upon his brother: and he sought where to weep; and he entered into his chamber, and wept there. And he washed his face, and went out, and refrained himself, and said, Set on bread. And they set on for him by himself, and for them by themselves, and for the Egyptians, which did eat with him, by themselves: because the Egyptians might not eat bread with the Hebrews; for that is an abomination unto the Egyptians. And they sat

before him, the firstborn according to his birthright, and the youngest according to his youth: and the men marveled one at another. And he took and sent messes unto them before him: but Benjamin's mess was five times so much as any of theirs. And they drank and were merry with him. (Gen. 43:24–34)

    The brothers and their donkeys are provided for. When Zaphnathpaaneah arrives, they give him their present. They bow to the earth before him once again. This time, it's all eleven.
    Joseph asks whether his father is still living. He is. He asks whether this is their youngest brother with them. He is.
    "God be gracious unto thee my son." Joseph speaks through an interpreter. The brothers wonder how on earth this ruler of Egypt knows anything about God the Father.
    Joseph has to excuse himself. He leaves and enters a separate room to weep. He gathers himself and returns. He orders lunch served. The brothers notice that every order he gives is carried out. Joseph is by himself at his own table. Did it irk him to be closest to Ruben and furthest from Benjamin? He has more food set before Benjamin. The brothers are having a wonderful time. It looks like nothing could go wrong!

Chapter 7

> And he commanded the steward of his house, saying, Fill the men's sacks with food, as much as they can carry, and put every man's money in his sack's mouth. And put my cup, the silver cup, in the sack's mouth of the youngest, and his corn money. And he did according as Joseph had spoken. As soon as the morning was light, the men were sent away, they and their asses. (Gen. 44:1–3)

The reunion, and then a trick! I was waiting for this! Revenge! It's exactly what I would have done. Accuse them of something they hadn't done, then catch them at it, and throw them in prison. Lock them up for life! They deserve it.

But is that what Joseph is doing? Or is this a test? Joseph was hated by his brothers because of his favored treatment. They had sold him as a slave. Would they be just as happy to rid themselves of their father's new favorite, Benjamin? Would they be happy to leave him in Egypt too? Joseph wanted to find out whether his brothers had changed.

"He commanded—," think about that. Think about what the brothers had intended for Joseph versus what had taken place. Joseph was giving orders to all Egyptians, not just the steward of his house. Joseph ordered the generals of Pharaoh's army. He ordered the steward to fill his brother's sacks, refund their money, and place his silver cup in Benjamin's sack. It was done! In the morning, his brothers left the home of this great man of Egypt. What an important, wise, powerful, but very strange Egyptian, was this Zaphnathpaanea! Why had they been his guests for lunch, they out of all the other people of all nations who had been in those long lines for food? And they were already packed and leaving! He had even seen to it that their donkeys were fed. It just didn't make sense!

Are Joseph's brothers brain dead? These things must have been on their minds as they began their 240-mile trip homeward. What did they think? Judah was no doubt relieved. He had purchased food. He had gotten Simeon released. He had Benjamin close to him. He was headed home a great success. But he had to wonder, *Why had this great ruler of Egypt been so gracious?* What a curious turn of events. Might there have been just a brief regret over his treatment of Joseph twenty two years ago? But then, the story isn't about Judah. The story isn't about Joseph either.

> And when they were gone out of the city, and not yet far off, Joseph said to his steward, Up, follow after the men; and when thou dost overtake them, say unto them, Wherefore have ye rewarded evil for good? Is not this it in which my lord drinketh, and whereby indeed he divineth? Ye have done evil in so doing. And he overtook them, and he spake unto them these same words. And they said unto him, Wherefore saith my lord these words? God forbid that thy servants should do according to this thing: Behold, the money, which we found in our sacks' mouths, we brought again unto thee out of the land of Canaan: how then should we steal out of thy lord's house silver or gold? With whomsoever of thy servants it be found, both let him die, and we also will be my lord's bondmen. And he said, Now also let it be according unto your words: he with whom it is found shall be my servant; and ye shall be blameless. Then they speedily took down every man his sack to the ground, and opened every man his sack. And he searched, and began at the eldest, and left at the youngest: and the cup was found

> in Benjamin's sack. Then they rent their clothes, and laded every man his ass, and returned to the city. (Gen. 44:4–13)

Just outside the city, what had to be Judah's incredible joy turned instantly to unimaginable fright. This was the chief steward of Zaphnathpaaneah! Judah thinks, *Why does he look so stern? What is this ridiculous accusation he is bringing? Rewarding evil for good? What? Us? Never! It's preposterous!*

Think back twenty-two years men. What had Joseph done? He did what his father had asked him to do. And what was that? To check on his brothers well-being and to check on you Judah. Was that good or evil? You say it was good, Judah? And how did you reward him? With evil, you admit it! So then, you rewarded evil for good just as the steward is saying. Isn't that right? Oh, I see, but this time you're innocent.

The steward completes the search, and Zaphnathpaaneah's cup is found in Benjamin's sack, right where Joseph had ordered it placed. The brothers reload their donkeys and head back to the city. Can you imagine how they felt on this trip? They face death or life as slaves, or worse, having to return home and face their father without Benjamin!

> And Judah and his brethren came to Joseph's house; for he was yet there: and they fell before him on the ground. And Joseph said unto them, "What deed is this that ye have done? Wot ye not that such a man as I can certainly divine?" (Gen. 44:14–15)

Okay, I get it. Joseph's dream came true in threes! His brethren spend more time staring at the ground than doing anything else with this ruler! Can you imagine their fear? How horrible can life get? They had to be thinking that! Never to see home again, their wives, and their children. Judah had grandchildren and great grandchildren. Torture? Prison? Dad's heartbreak. There are things worse than death.

> And Judah said, What shall we say unto my lord? What shall we speak? Or how shall we clear ourselves? God hath found out the iniquity of thy servants: behold, we are my lord's servants, both we, and he also with whom the cup was found. And he said God forbid that I should do so: but the man in whose hand the cup is found, he shall be my servant; and as for you, get you up in peace unto your father. (Gen. 44:16–17)

Finally! Judah is beginning to see! He connects his plight with his own sin. He understands consequences. He confesses. I know he left out a lot of detail, but he's scared to death, and this important man doesn't have time for details. If Judah only knew. He volunteers to be a servant. Joseph says, "No thanks. You can go free. I'm keeping Benjamin."

Chapter 8
The Intercession

Then Judah came near unto him, and said, Oh my lord, let thy servant, I pray thee, speak a word in my lord's ears, and let not thine anger burn against thy servant: for thou art even as Pharaoh. My lord asked his servants, saying Have ye a father or a brother? And we said unto my lord, We have a father, an old man, and a child of his old age, a little one; and his brother is dead, and he alone is left of his mother, and his father loveth him. And thou sadist unto thy servants, Bring him down unto me, that I may set my eyes upon him. And we said unto my lord, The lad cannot leave his father: for if he should leave his father, his father would die. And thou saidst unto thy servants, Except your youngest brother come down with you, ye shall see my face no more. And it came to pass when we came up to thy servant my father, we told him the words of my lord. And our father said, Go again, and buy us a little food. And we said, We cannot go down: if our youngest brother be with us, then will we go down: for we may not see the man's face except our youngest brother be with us. And thy servant my father said unto us, Ye know that my wife bare me two sons: And the one went out from me, and I said, surly he is

> torn in pieces; and I saw him not since: And if ye take this also from me, and mischief befall him, ye shall bring down my gray hairs with sorrow to the grave. Now therefore when I come to thy servant my father, and the lad be not with us; seeing that his life is bound up in the lad's life; It shall come to pass, when he seeth that the lad is not with us, that he will die: and thy sevants shall bring down the gray hairs of thy servant our father with sorrow to the grave. For thy servant became surety for the lad unto my father, saying, If I bring him not unto thee, then I shall bear the blame to my father for ever. Now therefore, I pray thee, let thy servant abide instead of the lad a bondman to my lord; and let the lad go up with his brethren. For how shall I go up to my father, and the lad be not with me? Lest peradventure I shall see the evil that shall come on my father. (Gen. 44:18–34)

Judah is a changed man. Twenty-two years ago, Joseph heard a different sounding Judah. Joseph was in a pit. He heard Judah say, "What profit is it if we slay our brother and conceal his blood? Come, let us sell him." But now, when confronted with the opportunity to be rid of another of his father's favorites, Judah reacts differently.

"Let thy servant, I pray thee, speak a word in my Lord's ears." Where is Ruben? Don't you wonder if he's even listening? Can he dare look up if his head is bowed? Can he see Judah speaking and the Egyptian ruler listening intently? What does a real leader say? Ruben must wonder. Ruben would be pleading, "Have pity on me! Think about what it will be like for me to have to tell my father this!"

Judah intercedes for his apparently guilty brother. Judah speaks lovingly of his father. He tells of the grief his father experienced while imagining the violent death Joseph must have suffered. Judah didn't entertain the possibility that Joseph might still be alive. "His (Benjamin's) brother (Joseph) is dead."

Judah describes what transpired at home with his father when they discussed the necessity of returning to Egypt with Benjamin in order to be able to purchase grain. His father had resisted. Finally, with the family facing starvation, Judah's father had allowed Benjamin to make the trip.

And here is one of the most beautiful passages of scripture in God's Word. Judah reasons with the Egyptian ruler. "When I come to thy servant my father, and the lad be not with us, he will die." Judah continues, "I became surety for the lad. Now therefore, I pray thee, let thy servant (me Judah) abide instead of the lad a bondman to my lord; and let the lad go with his brethren."

That's how you do it, Ruben! That's leadership. That's self sacrifice. That's interceding on someone's behalf. Now your sons don't have to be killed by their grandfather as you offered.

Chapter 9
The Reunion

> Then Joseph could not refrain himself before all them that stood by him; and he cried, Cause every man to go out from me. And there stood no man with him, while Joseph made himself known unto his brethren. And he wept aloud: and the Egyptians and the house of Pharaoh heard. And Joseph said unto his brethren, I am Joseph; doth my father yet live? And his brethren could not answer him; for they were troubled at his presence. And Joseph said unto his brethren, Come near to me, I pray you. And they came near. And he said, I am Joseph your brother, whom ye sold into Egypt. (Gen. 45: 1–4)

Joseph can't bear to hear more. Judah has been transformed during these twenty two years. He is no longer the jealous, hateful, vengeful, and greedy brother who had Joseph sold as a slave. He has offered himself to be a slave! Joseph may wonder why the fourth oldest brother is in charge, but if he does, he doesn't say so. He can't refrain himself. He commands all Egyptians to leave. He is now alone with his brothers. He cries so loudly that the Egyptians hear, as do the house of Pharaoh.

"I am Joseph, is my father still alive?" Joseph, until this point, only spoke to his brothers in Egyptian and through an interpreter. Now, for the first time, he is speaking Hebrew. "Come near to me."

It reminds me of Jesus saying to Thomas, "Reach hither thy finger, and behold my hands" (John 20:27).

Joseph's brothers are dumbfounded. They don't speak. They can't speak! They have no answer for him. The Bible says, "They were troubled at his presence." I'll just bet they were! They were silent. Joseph has to announce who he is a second time. He reminds them that he is the one they sold into slavery in Egypt twenty two years ago.

> Now therefore be not grieved, nor angry with yourselves, that ye sold me hither: for God did send me before you to preserve life." (Gen. 45:5)

This is one of the most profound declarations ever uttered by a man. It reveals a heart with deep faith and pure trust in God. This man, who above all other men of the Bible appears to be forsaken by God, declares that God has ordered his steps. While facing those who had sold him as a slave and caused him to be in prison for thirteen years and separated from his family for twenty two years, he implores, "…be not grieved nor angry with yourselves that ye sold me."

What does that sound like to you? Luke 23:34 perhaps? "Father forgive them for they know not what they do."

Joseph continues, "For God did send me before you to preserve life." The question is, whose life? It's true, God did send Joseph to Egypt to preserve life. But Joseph doesn't have any idea whose life God was preserving! The name of that person was not mentioned in the story. It was someone the reader of this Bible story can't know at this point.

Chapter 2
Judah and Tamar

Chapter 38 in the book of Genesis has been treated like a rude parenthetical insertion in the story of Joseph's life for much of the history of Christianity. Since the Bible was made available to common man, this chapter has been ignored as if it is a misplaced mistake. Many presentations of the story of "the Coat of Many Colors" or "Joseph in Egypt" leave it out altogether. After all, it's an absolute embarrassment!

You have the Lord slaying people, the head of the tribe from which the Messiah would eventually come, paying for a prostitute, a man performing coitus interruptus with his brother's wife in order to protect his own inheritance, and a woman pretending to be a whore and becoming pregnant by her father-in-law, is that enough? I am old. I have never heard Genesis chapter 38 preached from the pulpit. Pastors seem hard-pressed to find any redeeming value in it. No wonder it has been left out of what looks like, on the surface, to be Joseph's story. I'm going to have to ask you to sit down. The story isn't about Joseph!

In the book of Genesis, from the time Joseph is given the coat of many colors until he reveals his identity to his brothers in Egypt, the most significant piece of information is found in chapter 38. This same chapter that has been left out of so many accounts of "Joseph's story" is almost the whole story. I say "almost" because the person the story is about isn't mentioned in chapter 38 either.

I am so tempted to let you figure it out for yourself. It took me several decades of Bible study and teaching to finally "get it." Maybe

I'm just slow. Maybe you already know. First of all, let me reassure those of you who are afraid God might have made a mistake inspiring Moses to stick an unrelated chapter in this story, He didn't! Let's look at it and see how it's connected.

Genesis 38:1 says, "And it came to pass at that time." At what time? Don't just assume you know. You have to compare scripture with scripture to answer this question. What had just happened? In chapter 37 verse 36, Joseph had just been purchased by Potiphar. Joseph had only been in Egypt a matter of days. From examining other scripture, we discover the events related to chapter 38 span approximately forty eight years. Twenty-six of those years occur before Joseph is sold as a slave and twenty-two years occur after he was sold. We will cover these years later. What you need to understand is that a very significant thing in chapter 38 takes place close to the time Joseph was sold as a slave.

Judah takes a Canaanite woman for a wife. She conceives and has a son named Er. That same woman bears Judah two more sons, Onan and Shelah. Judah then takes Tamar as a wife for Er. Now he didn't kidnap her any more than he had "taken" his own wife. He simply approved of her. Er does some wicked thing the Bible doesn't record. God slays Er. We don't know what Er did nor how God killed him. He must have been really bad though because God didn't do that often.

Judah tells his second son to "go in unto thy brother's wife and raise up seed to thy brother." If Onan were to do that, the child that would be born would become an heir to Onan's father's wealth, and Onan would get less. The child would belong to Er, not Onan. Onan thinks about this and decides it would be best to ignore what Dad suggested and not get Tamar pregnant. He wasn't so convicted that he didn't want to have sex with Tamar, only that he didn't want her to get pregnant. I guess we can classify him as "partially convicted." So did God. God slew Onan too. Judah tells Tamar to go home and live with her father until Shelah, Judah's youngest son, is old enough to marry, or at least raise up seed to Er.

Judah's own wife dies. Judah takes a trip to have his sheep sheared. I've done that. That's what you do with sheep. You sell their wool to make money. Tamar finds out about the trip and devises a plan. Poor Tamar is frustrated. She got married. Her husband died. She has no children (especially sons), and she's getting concerned about her future. There will be no one to take care of her in her old age. Don't be too upset with Tamar. That's just the way things were back then. Here's her plan, she will put a veil over her face, pretend to be a prostitute, and make certain Judah sees her on his trip with the sheep. She wants to trick him like this because he reneged on his promise to have Shelah marry her.

Judah falls for it and wants sex with this woman he doesn't realize is his daughter-in-law. Tamar isn't stupid. She negotiates a payment. Judah promises her a kid out of the flock. The kids are not on this trip with him. He brought only adult sheep to be sheared. Now Tamar doesn't want a kid out of the flock any more than you do. So she informs Judah she wants something for security, which she will return to Judah when she gets the kid.

Judah asks, "What do you want?"

I feel as though I have to interject something here. Men can be so stupid when it comes to sex. It's as though they think with something other than their brain. Judah is about to really mess up.

Tamar answers, "Please give me everything you have on you that will allow me to positively identify you as the father in a future paternity lawsuit." Well, she doesn't say those exact words, but that's exactly what she means.

Judah says, after very little thought, "Okay." He gives her his staff, ring, and bracelets and has sex with her. He has no idea it's Tamar. When he returns home, he sends a servant with a kid from the flock to pay the prostitute and get his "stuff" back. Of course, "the prostitute" is nowhere to be found.

Three months later, Tamar is reported to be "with child by whoredom." Judah says, "No problem. Bring her forth and let her be burned." Men fetch Tamar, and before she makes the trip to be burned at the stake, she decides it might be best to bring Judah's "stuff" with her. She quickly produces her "evidence," and I picture the men scurrying around trying to put out the fire. Judah is especially embarrassed.

Tamar goes back home and has twin sons (Pharez and Zarah). This is the significant event, which takes place as Joseph arrives in Egypt as a slave.

Lets add this up:

- Judah gets married—one year
- Judah's wife has three sons—three years
- Er grows up and gets married—twenty years
- Er and Onan died—one year
- Tamar waits for Shelah—one year
- Tamar is pregnant and gives birth to twins—one year
- We know from Genesis 46:12 that Pharez grows up and gets married—twenty years
- Pharez's wife has two sons who travel with Jacob to Egypt—two years
- Total of forty-nine years

The last twenty-two years of that chronology took place while Joseph was a slave in Egypt. So while "at that time" in Genesis 38:1 refers to Joseph's journey to Egypt, what happened at that time was the birth of Pharez. Pharez then grew up, got married, and had two sons while Joseph was in Egypt. We know this because he shows up in Egypt with two sons as Genesis 46:12 states, "And the sons of Pharez were Hezron and Hamul."

Let's add the years of Joseph in Egypt.

- Joseph is sold to Potiphar at age seventeen (Gen.37:1).
- He gets out of prison at age thirty—thirteen years (Gen. 41:46).
- The seven years of plenty ended—seven years (Gen. 41:53).
- Two years of famine pass before Joseph reveals his identity to his brothers—two years (Gen. 45:6).
- Total of twenty-two yrs.

Joseph is 39 years old when Jacob and the rest of his family come to live in Egypt. Jacob is 130 years old (Gen. 47:9). Benjamin could be as old as 38 years but can't be much younger than 30 because he has ten sons (Gen. 46:21). Pharez is 22 years old and his sons are close to two and one. Pharez's sons were Hezron and Hamul (Gen. 46:12).

Famines are natural disasters that take a cruel toll of human life. They are especially hard on three groups of people. The sick don't do well. Whether they are deteriorating or healing, the sick need excellent nutrition, which is not available during a famine. The elderly don't do well. Older people are running down in the best of conditions and famines merely speed that process. Finally, infants don't do well. Mother's milk dries up, parents become tired more easily without food, and infants end up with less care and poorer nutrition than they need to survive. People die during famines. Even healthy people die. But the infirm, elderly, and young die at a faster rate.

Man's Fall and God's Solution

Wow! That's going back a bit. Both Adam and Eve disobey God in the Garden of Eden (Gen. 3:6). God was not pleased with Adam and Eve and was less pleased with the serpent who beguiled them. God devised a plan to redeem fallen man right then. Genesis 3:15 says, "And I (God) will put enmity between thee (Satan) and the woman, and between thy seed (Satan's) and her seed (eventually Jesus)." God began the process of bringing the Messiah into the world right there in the Garden.

In Luke 3:23, the genealogy of Christ's family is given. Heli was Mary's father. Luke doesn't say Heli begat Joseph (Mary's husband). He didn't. Jacob was Joseph's biological father (Matt. 1:16). Heli was Joseph's father-in-law. He was simply the "legal" father of Joseph. The genealogies in Matthew 1 and Luke 3 are Christ's genealogies through both Joseph and Mary. Christ wasn't related to Joseph biologically but even Joseph had a connection to David, Judah, Jacob, and Abraham as was prophesied for the Messiah.

Let's go to both of those genealogies and look who is mentioned at the time of the famine while Joseph (son of Jacob) was in Egypt. Matthew 1:3 says, "And Judas (Greek for Judah) begat Phares

(Greek for Pharez) and Zara (Greek for Zarah) of Thamar (Greek for Tamar) and Phares begat Esrom (Greek for Hezron)." Luke 3:33 says, "Which was the son of Esrom, (Hezron) which was the son of Phares, (Pharez) which was the son of Juda (another Greek form of Judah)."

So the Messianic bloodline that had started in the Garden of Eden with Adam went through the young boy, Hezron, who was brought to Egypt to live during the last five years of the famine, which had devastated Canaan where he lived. He was most likely between the ages one and two when he arrived in Egypt. My guess is that he was malnourished.

Now pay attention. This isn't mentioned in the Bible, this is just me using logic. For God to successfully execute the plan He related to Satan in the Garden of Eden concerning the coming Messiah, He does not need Jacob at the time of the famine. Jacob could have died, and it would not have thwarted God's plan one iota because Jacob had begotten Judah. God likewise didn't need Judah because Judah had begotten Pharez of Tamar. He didn't need Pharez because Pharez had begotten Hezron. But Hezron was important. God needed to get food into Hezron. Hezron was the current end of the Messianic bloodline. Jacob, Judah, Pharez, Joseph, Joseph's other brothers, Pharaoh, all the people who are mentioned by name between Genesis 37:1 and Genesis 45:3 could have died in the famine, and it would not have altered God's plan for mankind's redemption. But not so with Hezron. Everything that happened to Joseph in Dothan and in Egypt had to do with getting food for Hezron.

Chapter 10
You

I said this book was about you. You have thought this book was about Joseph. You think your life is about you, where you were born, where you have lived, where you go, what you study, where you work, your role in your family, who you will marry, where you take your kids, how you deal with your problems, what God thinks of you, what sins easily beset you, and what kind of a Christian or non-Christian (I hope not) you are. You think that I, this book, God, Jesus, your family, your friends, your coworkers, and all the places you go and things that are around you are part of "your story." You do. I know you do. We all do. It's only natural. We do it with Bible characters. We think there is a different story about Adam, Noah, Abraham, Isaac, Jacob, Joseph, Moses, Joshua, David, and so on. There isn't. It's all one story.

I hate to pop your "life's all about me" bubble, but it isn't about you! "Joseph's story" wasn't about him either. The story was more about Hezron than Joseph, and Hezron isn't even mentioned in it! But it wasn't Hezron's story either. Don't you see? The story is God's story. I know what you're thinking. Well if it's God's story, why doesn't he exercise a little better control over it?

If I had been in control, I would have had Joseph speak to his father reasonably. "Dad, there's no reason I can't work in the fields with my brothers. Please let me go. This coat is truly beautiful, but none of my older brothers have anything like it, and I don't want to make them feel badly." Then his brothers wouldn't have sold him as a slave. I also would have prevented the famine from happening at all. Hezron would have been in no danger. The Messianic bloodline would have been under no risk of ending.

But during my life, 3,700 years later, when I experienced difficulties, I would have wrongly concluded that God didn't care enough about me to prevent bad things from happening to me. As my life went on, I'd become convinced God didn't love me. But I have no such delusion! God is sovereign and can do as He pleases, and it is always best. God shows me He is with me every step of the way. I can face adversity without fear. I can experience the worst of life's difficulties, believing I am loved by God the Father, Creator of the universe!

I haven't lived on earth for very much of God's story. But I have seen many natural disasters. I have never seen God intervene to stop a natural disaster. He may have, but how would I know? Natural disasters occur, and the ones that have happened in my life, God didn't stop. Earthquakes, tsunamis, storms, famines, and floods have all happened as God chose not to intervene. God didn't stop the famine that threatened to end the Messianic bloodline, which would have occurred with the death of Hezron either. But God allowed the actions of men to bring about a good result in spite of the famine and in spite of men's evil intentions.

God tells us by the hand of Moses that He "sent" Joseph to Egypt. But as we have discovered, only Hezron needed to be spared. All the rest merely benefited from what was happening to Hezron. Moses himself was a decedent of one of Levi's three sons.

How is this related to you? How do you see your life? Is your life complicated? Have there been people in your life that have treated you unfairly? Have people been mean to you? Have you been victimized by favoritism? Have you been victimized by jealousy? Have you ever been falsely accused of doing something you actually took a strong stand against? Have siblings lied to your parents about you? All those things happened to Joseph, and yet he states, "God did send me before you to preserve life."

Let's examine your life more closely. Why did you pick up this book? Have you been overworked by an employer? Have you been underpaid? Have you been misunderstood by family or friends? Have you suffered punishment for things you didn't do? Are you underappreciated at church? Have you ever been cut off by other drivers in traffic? Have you been splashed by a truck while walking as a pedestrian? Have you been rained on when you weren't prepared? Have you lost property in a storm? Have you lost money in the stock market? Have you ever been sick? Are you still sick? Do you suffer from a debilitating disease? Are you in an abusive relationship? Would you describe your life as a "living Hell?" or is your life an endless routine?

Have you prayed for the same thing for a long time? How long? A year? Five years? Ten? If Joseph prayed for God to get him out of prison, it took thirteen years. The Bible doesn't record that he prayed for that at all. He may have, but the Bible doesn't confirm that he did. More to the point, did God reveal his purpose to Joseph? He certainly didn't reveal His specific purpose. What exactly did God do? He did the same thing He has done throughout the history of man. God equipped Joseph to accomplish God's will! You and I go through life, praying that God will accomplish our will. Admit it. That's what we do. Is it any wonder we become frustrated by what appears to be God's disinterest?

The creator of the universe, God the Father of our Lord and Savior Jesus Christ, loves you! He provided for you in eternity past. What are your problems again? If you have the suspicion that God is too busy to care about you and your problems, you are suffering from a delusion. Satan has given you that absurd impression. God, on the other hand, has done everything in history on your behalf!

I am now halfway through my fifth decade of teaching God's Word and counseling Christians of all ages and walks of life. I've heard the saddest stories you can imagine. Perhaps yours is sadder. I have sad stories of my own. None of these stories hinder what God has been doing since man's fall in the Garden of Eden. Adam and Eve made a mistake. We should get on our knees and thank them for it! It resulted in the most beautiful plan imaginable. God provided for the redemption of mankind! That's you! Look, I'm not minimizing your problems, whatever they are. They may be the worst I've ever heard, but God brought Jesus into this world to negate the ending Satan wants for you. He started with Adam. Don't you see? The bloodline went through Hezron! Then came Jesus!

Perhaps you are praying for "benefits." What kind of benefits are you hoping for? The Christian life shouldn't be about benefits for believers. It is about God's will and your part in it. God wasn't finally giving Joseph a wonderful life to make up for how crappy his life had been. What God did by making Joseph ruler of Egypt was for you! Don't you get it? Joseph getting out of prison and being elevated in status by Pharaoh had zero to do with God, wanting to bless Joseph for the suffering he had experienced.

God has a will. It will not be thwarted. We can make ourselves available to God to assist Him in accomplishing His will or not. God doesn't decide that. You do. Ruben had a chance. He had two or three chances. He missed his opportunities. Ruben cared more about Ruben than anyone or anything else. Perhaps he learned. The Bible doesn't say.

The far more important question is, have you learned? Don't think I'm scolding you for praying your problems would go away or at least subside. What you have to realize is that God accomplishing His will doesn't depend on that. You can be a factor in God accomplishing His will in spite of your continuing problems. More importantly, you must see by now that God has not abandoned you.

You're thinking, *Well where was God when all of these troubles overtook me?* I'll tell you where He was, and the Lord was with (fill in your name). He most certainly has never abandoned you.

A story will one day be told about someone else. You will be in it. What part will you play? Will you be a jealous sibling? Will you be a poor leader? Will you go through life, wondering where God is when you really need Him, or will the hand of God upon you be evident to others? You get to decide, no one else.

God wasn't punishing Joseph for his sins in the story. Joseph was tactless and shared his dreams of ruling over his family with all of them. He also wore his beautiful (Daddy loves me most) coat in front of his brothers. He suffered consequences for his tactlessness. Consequences come in many forms. A child out of wedlock is a consequence for sinful behavior. The child is not a punishment.

Addiction is a consequence of drug use, not a punishment. AIDS is a consequence. Broken marriages are consequences. Disease is a consequence. The point is, we don't pay God for our sins. Jesus paid it all! He paid the entire price. Consequences we suffer are no indication we have been abandoned by God. God loves you! He sent His Son Jesus to die for you. Trusting in Christ's shed blood's ability to wash away your sin and belief in His resurrection brings you God's forgiveness.

Jacob, Judah, Tamar, Ruben, Potiphar's wife, Pharaoh, Joseph, Hezron, and many others had a hand in God's plan to redeem you. Isn't it time you stopped whining and complaining? A happy carefree life with no people or circumstantial problems is not evidence that God is "with" you. He is simply with you. If God directed Joseph's life in such a complicated way to bring about such a good result, can't He work in yours? And what was the good result? The redemption of mankind! And now He doesn't care about you? Does that make any sense? Can't you see how ridiculous that is?

God loves you! He sent Jesus to die in your place. You have the promise of eternity with Him. And you believe God has abandoned you? Guess again!

Appendix A
Joseph, a Type of Christ

Similarities	Joseph	Christ
Large family with brothers and sisters	Genesis 34:1 Genesis 35:22	Mark 6:3
Honored by his father	Genesis 37:3	Luke 3:22
Claims he will rule over his parents	Genesis 37:5	Luke 2:49
Obedient to his father in a hard task	Genesis 37:14	Hebrews 12:2
Goes the distance after a pause	Genesis 37:17	Luke 22:42 John 19:17
Brothers conspire to kill him	Genesis 37: 18	Luke 20:19
Not respected by his own kin	Genesis 37:19	Mark 6:4
Stripped of his robe	Genesis 37:23	Mark 15:20
Cast into a pit	Genesis 37:24	Mark 15:46
Wounded in the house of his friends	Genesis 37:24	Zechariah 13:6
Betrayed and sold for the price of a slave by a man named Judah/Judas	Genesis 37:28	Matthew 26:15

Fled to Egypt to escape from those who wanted him dead	Genesis 37:28	Matthew 2:13
Resurrected from the grave	Genesis 37:28	Matthew 28:6
Vesture dipped in blood	Genesis 37:31	Revelation 19:13
Had to "die" before he could save	Genesis 37:32–33	Mark 8:31
He was falsely accused.	Genesis 39:17–18	Mark 14:56-59 Matthew 26:59–60
The Lord was with him.	Genesis 39:21	John 4:32
Interpreted parables	Genesis 40:12, 18	Matthew 13:18
Authorities marvel at his doctrine	Genesis 41:38	Luke 2:47
Thirty years old when he began his ministry	Genesis 41:46	Luke 3:23
Fed the multitudes	Genesis 41:55–57	Matthew 14:19
Both wept	Genesis 42:24	John 11:35
He said, "Come to me."	Genesis 45:4	Matthew 11:28
Forgiving of those who mistreated him	Genesis 45:5	Luke 23:34
No sins are recorded for him.		Hebrews 4:15
Many came to see him.	Genesis 47:14–26	Matthew 8:1
Both were detained with two others who were condemned to die. One was pardoned and given life.	Genesis 40:21–22	Luke 23:39–43

All knees bow to Joseph and will bow to Jesus.	Genesis 47:25	Romans 14:11
Brothers don't honor him but later reconciled	Genesis 45:15 Genesis 34:1	John 7:5 Acts 1:13-14
Spoke not in own defense	Genesis 39:19	Matthew 27:12

Appendix B
Joseph Study

Day 1

You are about to begin a study of the life of Jacob's son, Joseph. You may think you know all about him, but do you know what God is saying to you about you in the story of Joseph?

This study might serve as a shortcut for you. If you discover what God wants you to understand about your relationship with Him by examining the circumstances of Joseph's life, it will improve yours.

Are there problems that trouble you in life? Does life seem unfair? Does your life sometimes seem like a hopeless jumble of totally unrelated events? Perhaps your life is more like a routine that seems endless. Are you in a rut? Are the sides of that rut getting deeper? Do you cry out to God for deliverance and get no answer?

Do this daily study and pray that God will open your eyes to the truth of His love for you.

Today's assignment: Just pray. Pray the Holy Spirit will guide you to the truth of God's Word.

Your thoughts:

_____
_____
_____
_____

FOOD FOR HEZRON

_____
_____
_____
_____
_____
_____

Day 2

In the eighteenth century BC, there was a family living near Mount Hebron, 2,800 feet above sea level, twenty miles west of the Dead Sea. The family consisted of a husband, one of his two wives (one had died giving birth to his twelfth son), his wives' two handmaids, the twelve sons born to those four women, and an unknown number of sisters. The husband's name was Jacob.

Long before he was married, Jacob had been asked by his father to simply speak his true name. He lied (Genesis 27:18–19). Jacob lied in order to receive a blessing from his father that rightly belonged to his older twin brother, Esau. Jacob's father was fooled as he was old and blind (Genesis 27:1). The lie Jacob told led to the breakup of his family and a long estrangement from his twin brother who had vowed to kill Jacob (Genesis 27:41).

Today's assignment: Read Proverbs 6:16–17

What does God think of lying?
_____
_____
_____

Always? _____
So you think you might enjoy better circumstances if you were honest always? _____

Pray the Holy Spirit would convict you of any tendency to be dishonest.

Day 3

More than twenty years later (Genesis 31:38), Jacob was about to come into the company of his brother, Esau, for the first time since their breakup (Genesis 32:6). Jacob was certain Esau would still want to kill him as he did when they had parted. On the eve of that reunion until sunrise, Jacob wrestled with a being who did not identify himself. We learn from the prophet Hosea (12:4) that Jacob had wrestled with an angel, a messenger from God. These many years Jacob had been living as though he were Esau. His father had given Jacob Esau's blessing because of the lie he had told. Jacob was enjoying a life enriched by a blessing he had stolen from his brother. God hadn't forgotten. For more than twenty years, God had watched Jacob living a lie. While he wrestles the angel, Jacob threatens to hold the angel until he blesses Jacob. It is so interesting that instead of just saying no, God (speaking through the angel messenger) demands that Jacob identifies himself. He says, "What is thy name?" The last time he had been asked that question, he had lied. This time, he doesn't. He says, "Jacob." God says, "Thy name shall be called no more Jacob but Israel" (Genesis 32:28, 35:10). So out of truth, we have the birth of the nation Israel, God's people.

Today's assignment: A lie brought the destruction of a family. Truth brought the birth of a nation. Jacob got a second chance after twenty years of living a lie.

You have a second chance immediately after telling a lie. You also have a second chance after telling a lie no matter how long it has been.

There are a number of different ways of being dishonest. Is there any area in your life where you are less than honest?

_____
_____
_____
_____
_____

Pray God gives you the courage to correct your lies of the past and to be truthful in your interactions with others from now on.

Day 4

Sins are often repeated in subsequent generations of families. Psychologists tell us that children who are abused by their parents often commit the same abuses on their own children. This happens often in our experience, and here is a biblical example. Isaac had shown favoritism toward Esau. His wife, Rebekah, favored Jacob (Genesis 25:28). It was this favoritism that had led to the destruction of Isaac's family. Rebekah orders her favorite son to stay "a few days" with her brother to keep Jacob safe from Esau. "A few days" turns into 7,300 days (Genesis 31:38). What's more, Rebekah never lays eyes on Jacob again in his life!

So the last person you would expect to see showing favoritism is Jacob. He had seen it pit him against his brother, cause him to lie to his father, and separate him from his mother forever on this earth. But by the time we learn of Joseph's early life, we find that he too is a victim of favoritism committed by Jacob (Genesis 37:3).

Today's assignment: Think about your own memories of childhood. Can you remember actual words spoken to you by your parents? Probably not unless those words were often repeated sayings. But you can undoubtedly remember things your parents did.

I grew up in a non-Christian home where my father often said, "Do as I say, not as I do." But before I became a Christian, I had repeated every sin of my father. I thought he was good, and I wanted to be like him. I "learned" from what he did, not from what he said.

Parents need to realize their children learn far more from watching their parent's behavior than from hearing what parents say (Exodus 34:6–7).

Pray that the Holy Spirit would guide you to be a good example to those who watch you regardless of your relationship to them.

Day 5

In Genesis 37:1, we find Israel (Jacob) dwelling in what would eventually become the Promised Land. But Jacob doesn't realize that his family is the nation of Israel or that they currently occupy the place where Joshua would lead the nation of Israel several hundred years later. The family lives on the northern slopes of Mount Hebron. Joseph is seventeen years old, and his younger brother Benjamin is at home. Joseph was loved more than his older brothers by his father Israel (Genesis 37:3). Israel made this obvious to the older brothers by keeping Joseph home when he was certainly old enough to be working with his brothers as a shepherd. Israel made his own sin of favoritism even more obvious by giving Joseph a costly coat unlike anything his older brothers owned (Genesis 37:3). It should come as no surprise that Joseph's brothers hated him (Genesis 37:4).

Here is a great lesson for us all. Few friends and fewer siblings derive much pleasure from our good fortune when it comes to us at their expense. Can you imagine giving a present to your child on one of your other children's birthdays and not giving a gift to the child whose birthday it was? Who could do such a thing? Jacob did! Joseph's brothers hated him and had little respect for their father as we shall see.

Today's assignment: Read Genesis 37:1–4. Favoritism destroys morale among siblings and coworkers. Favoritism is different than rewarding good behavior or hard work. Showing favoritism is showing blessings toward children or subordinates in spite of their performance. Parents and employers who do this lose respect and ruin morale among their children and subordinates.

Have you ever experienced favoritism?

_____
_____
_____
_____
_____
_____
_____
_____
_____
_____

Pray that the Holy Spirit would convict you of any tendency to show favoritism where it can cause resentment.

Day 6

There are no sins recorded in scripture attributed to Joseph. We will discuss why that is later. It certainly can't be due to the possibility that Joseph never sinned. Joseph was a man. And all men have sinned (Romans 3:10, 23). Joseph also had one or two flaws in his character that were recorded. He seems to have lacked tact, and he was naive. After dreaming he would one day rule over his brothers and mother and father, he shares this news with them in the ultimate act of simplicity! What was he thinking? Did he expect them to believe it might happen and rejoice with him about it? If his announcement wasn't a sin, it was most certainly tactless and naïve. But you have to admit, he was honest.

Today's assignment: Is it ever right behavior to not express honesty? Absolutely yes! You hear your friend play an instrument. You've been playing the same instrument for many years, and you are *much* better than your friend. Your friend asks, "What do you think of my playing?" You say, "It made me want to throw up!" No, you don't! You exercise tact. If you don't you are mean and naive.

Now give an example from your experience.

Let's see, what should we pray about today? Pray that the Lord will make you sensitive to the feelings of people with whom you interact.

Day 7

In Genesis 37:12, we learn that Joseph's older brothers travel about forty-eight miles north to graze the flock in Shechem. Israel then calls Joseph and asks him to go ninety-six miles round trip just to check up on his brothers.

Just think of that in the context of our lives today. You have one son working outside and another inside, reading a book. (I say reading a book because I hope that son isn't playing a video game or watching television.) You ask the son who's reading the book to stop, put the book down, and go out and check on your other son to see how the work is going. How would your book reading son react? Now what if your working son was a quarter mile away on your farm? What if he was on the other side of your county? How about if he was forty-eight miles somewhere north of you in open country, grazing your farm animals? I know the answers to those questions, and so do you. I brought up my children in a Christian home with Christian values. They are wonderful Christians today, and they were a pleasure to live with while they were under my authority. But my book-reading child would let me know with facial expressions and body language that checking on a sibling in the backyard was an inconvenience. Traveling a quarter mile would have resulted in a request to reconsider. Going to the other side of the county would have resulted in an argument. And traveling forty-eight miles somewhere north would have resulted in a blank stare conveying the thought, *Dad's gone crazy!*

Don't be too quick to dismiss your child's probable behavior with "times are different now." I know they are. But children shouldn't be. What I really want you to grasp today is that Joseph is different! Why?

Today's assignment: What difficult task are you asked (or told) to do this week?
_____
_____
_____

What is your attitude?
_____
_____
_____

Tell you what, read Colossians 3:23–24. Now go live like that with a smile on your face!

Pray and thank the Lord for giving you an opportunity to be of use to Him in the kingdom.

Day 8

Seventeen hundred years or so after Joseph lived, Jesus is asked by His father to do a difficult thing. He goes to the cross willingly to die in pain there for you. The Old Testament is filled with "types" of Christ. These types illustrate some aspect of the Messiah's work. Why just in Genesis, we have the ark of Noah. There was only one door (Genesis 6:16), and you had to be in the ark to be saved. We also have the story of a ram caught in a thicket that became a substitute sacrifice for Isaac (Genesis 22:13). And now we have Joseph being obedient to his father and becoming a type of Christ. The Bible records no sins for Joseph. He had them of course, but scripture doesn't record them. And Joseph gives no back talk, no eye roll, just "Here am I" (Genesis 37:13). Jacob sent him, and he went. Christ goes to the cross as His father bid Him. It is a difficult trip, but in effect, He says,

"Here am I." That Joseph is a type of Christ will become even more obvious in the rest of this study. There are more than twenty ways.

Today's assignment: How Christlike are you in carrying out what you are asked to do in ministry?
_____
_____

How Christlike is your attitude toward your family?
_____
_____

Friends?
_____

Leaders?
_____

Subordinates?
_____

People to whom you minister?
_____

I know. Me too. We can't help it. We're sinners.
Pray and confess your sins. Pray for a heart that wants to make you more like Jesus.

Day 9

Well, after a forty-eight-mile trek north, Joseph arrives in the area where he expects to find his brothers. They're gone. A man tells Joseph they've traveled fifteen miles further north to Dothan (Genesis 37:17). So Joseph goes on a bit further after a brief pause.

He has now traveled sixty-three miles on this trip to satisfy his father's curiosity. I see in this pause a glimpse into the Messiah's life on earth. Jesus completes his preaching and healing ministry. He pauses in the Garden of Gethsemane (Matthew 22:42, John 19:17).

But now, see the terrible consequence of favoritism in a family (Genesis 37:18). Joseph's brothers conspire to kill him before they even learn why he has walked more than sixty miles to find them. He might be about to announce the death of their father. They don't know. What they do know is that they want Joseph dead. They even plan a lie to tell their father.

And how do they know it's Joseph? He's far off. It's that infernal coat! They hate that coat! They hate Joseph! And they don't think very much of their father. Joseph and his coat were constant reminders of their own ill favor in the eyes of their father. The coat must have brought to their minds Joseph's dreams of one day ruling over his family.

Today's assignment: Think of Paul. Paul was called by God to take the gospel to the Gentiles. After preaching for years, Paul describes his life (2 Corinthians 11:21–28). Now, is life fair? Paul ends up in prison and eventually beheaded. Is that fair?

What's not fair in your life?
_____
_____
_____

Don't look for fair. It doesn't happen! Do what God calls you to do. Just do it! Pray God will give you the courage. Everything will work out according to God's plan.

Day 10

Reuben, Jacob's firstborn (Genesis 29:32, 35:23), was in charge. If anything bad happened to Joseph, it would be Reuben's fault. Reuben's counterplot "appears" to be in concert with his brother's plans (Genesis 37:22). But his true motive is to save Joseph's life and keep his brothers from committing a horrible sin.

Reuben is in charge. He should be able to say, "You aren't going to do this!" That should be the end of it. But he doesn't. He sneaks. He's weak. He should have said, "You're going to have to kill me first."

These plans took considerable time to formulate. The brothers plotted as Joseph approached from "afar."

Today's assignment: What are your responsibilities? What do people expect from you?

_____
_____
_____
_____
_____

Don't fail to meet your responsibilities due to someone's alternative plan to sin instead. Most people want to follow a strong-willed person who is doing things God's way. Be that person. What if Reuben had said, "Listen to yourselves. Let's kill Joseph and tell father a lie. Then we'll ask God to bless that I suppose! Really?" What would they have done?

Pray you recognize and meet your responsibilities.

Day 11

We are such pathetic creatures! The objects of our hatred are often inanimate! Joseph's brothers can't stand the sight of that coat another second. When he arrives, they're going to tear it off him.

Let's get in Joseph's head for a minute. He sees the destination of his search for thirty minutes perhaps. He realizes they're his brothers before they recognize him. He is so excited! He hasn't seen them for days. He found them! It had been so disappointing when he hadn't found them in Shechem. He'd probably been wondering whether he'd find them in Dothan. But he sees them now. He's tired but excited. He covers these last two miles at a quicker pace. He can't wait to talk to them. He has news of his nieces and nephews.

But before he can get "Shalom" out of his mouth, he's on his back with his brothers on top of him! If any words are spoken, they are harsh words of hatred.

Violence against Joseph is planned. If Joseph speaks, they are screams of pleading. Only Reuben listens. He suggests casting Joseph into a nearby pit to rid Joseph out of his brothers' hands. Before they throw him in the pit, they strip off his beautiful coat. See Mark 15:20.

Today's assignment: Mob rule. Men will do in a mob what they would never do individually. Decisions like this always come down to a choice. The choice is always between right and wrong. Mobs often pick wrong.

Have you ever been negatively influenced by a group?
_____
_____
_____
_____
_____

Pray you will always be led by the Holy Spirit to do right. You may have to pay a great price to do right. But in the end, that price will be worth it. Picking wrong always leads to shame.

Day 12

Joseph is in the pit. He has been roughed up. His coat is gone. And his brothers sit down to have lunch! (Genesis 37:25).

Merchants were traveling from the east toward the southwest to go to Egypt. It is interesting that it is Judah, Leah's fourth son, who speaks about profit. "What profit is it if we slay our brother and conceal his blood?" (Genesis 37:26). Judah, the head of the tribe from which the Messiah would eventually come, had a worldly profit in mind for himself.

But the sparing of Joseph's life was to result in a spiritual profit that was intended by God for the benefit of all of mankind! The brothers eventually agree with Judah's plan, and Joseph is sold for the price of a slave (Matthew 26:15). Joseph is resurrected out of the pit (Matthew 28:6).

I have often wondered where Reuben was when Joseph was sold. Judah had no right to speak or lead his brothers. Simeon was next in line to be in charge in Reuben's absence. Where was he? Perhaps Reuben is tending the flock while his brothers eat. Leadership broke down.

The marine corps taught me many things about leadership. Don't order men to do what you wouldn't do. Lead by example. At the same time, don't try to do everything yourself. Become comfortable ordering others to do dangerous things. And no matter what is necessary to get the mission accomplished, do not endanger yourself simply because you don't want to endanger your men. Use your brain and give orders. Another lesson that is often learned the hard way is, recognize potential threats to your mission and neutralize them.

Reuben forgot that one. Escaping livestock was not the greatest threat to his mission. As the oldest, Reuben was not only in charge of sheep. He was in charge of his brothers. And his brothers had become the greatest threat to his mission. After learning of their plan to kill Joseph, how could Reuben have left Joseph alone with them? But he did. Reuben was a poor leader. That isn't my assessment. It's God's (Genesis 35:22, 49:3–4). His brothers neither respect him nor listen to him. They operate totally outside his leadership whether behind his back or to his face.

Today's assignment: Are you a leader or is it your job right now to follow one? Maybe you're both. Explain. How are you doing?

_____
_____
_____
_____

Pray about it!

FOOD FOR HEZRON

Day 13

Yesterday, we saw another interesting similarity in our story. Joseph was betrayed and sold for the price of a slave by someone you wouldn't suspect, a man close to him, a man named Judah. Christ was betrayed and sold for the price of a slave by someone you wouldn't suspect, a man close to him, a man named Judas. Judah and Judas were both one of a group of twelve. If that isn't an example of Old Testament typology, what is? (Genesis 37:28).

Joseph had to travel to Egypt to keep those who wanted him dead from killing him. His home wasn't far from Bethlehem. Does any of this sound at all familiar? Read Matthew 2:13. What a coincidence huh? Do you think maybe God has everything under control?

Poor Reuben returns. Nobody will listen to him. Notice that he doesn't say, "What are we going to do?" or "What is going to happen to Joseph?" Instead he verbalizes his innermost feelings, "And I, wither shall I go?" Poor Reuben. Poor baby. It makes me want to slap him! Sorry, that's the marine in me coming out. Maybe it's the Holy Spirit. Either way, I'd have slapped him! (Genesis 37:29–30).

Joseph's vesture is dipped in blood by "friends" from his own house (Genesis 37:31, Zechariah 13:6, Revelation 19:13). Wow!

Today's assignment: We are always in control of what we do. We are not in control of others nor the chance circumstances of life. Sometimes people around us simply need to be shown the right thing to do. They won't always do the right thing. But you should always show them the right thing. What are some "right things" you can show people today?

_____
_____
_____
_____

Pray for God to first reveal the right thing to you, then give you the boldness (and a good amount of humility) to show others the right thing. Reuben wishes he had done that!

Day 14

The lie is told (Genesis 37:32–35). The liar is lied to. Jacob had lied to his father, and now his sons are lying to him. Did they fake sorrow? Was their pulse rate high? Did they dare look at each other? Picture the utter hypocrisy of Jacob's sons trying to comfort him. Picture Reuben.

Sold for twenty pieces of silver. Two pieces each for the ten brothers. Joseph's younger brother Benjamin was still at home and not in on the lie. Had they already spent the money? Was any of it left? Did any of it jingle in their pockets when they hugged their father? What did they buy with it? What could you find comfort in owning by spending money you received for selling your brother? Could you buy something that would last that became a constant reminder? How I wonder what they did with that money!

Well, the descendants of Ishmael from Midian sold Joseph for much more than twenty pieces of silver. You can be certain of that! Potiphar, the captain of Pharaoh's palace police, purchased Joseph as a slave.

Ten brothers know the lie. Maybe some weren't as "guilty" as others. Maybe some didn't rough up Joseph or throw him in the pit. Perhaps some didn't take any of the silver. But all ten knew the lie. "Therefore to him that knoweth to do good, and doith it not, to him it is sin" (James 4:17). They were all guilty. "Lie not one to another" (Colossians 3:9).

Today's assignment: We've talked about lying before. It seems as though God is telling us to be truthful again. Is there something untruthful in our lives we aren't admitting? It's time to fix this. Actually, it's past time.

Pray. Maybe you'd better just pray about this matter rather than write anything down that someone might read. Remember, God already knows. But you still need to confess it.

Day 15

I am asking you to do something. Please indulge me in this request. We are going to skip chapter 38 and cover it later. When we do cover it later, the reason will be apparent. I will offer an observation here that I hope will satisfy the more curious among you.

For many years of my Christian life, the story of Joseph was told to me by those who thought they knew it. All of them excluded chapter 38 of Genesis. Chapter 38 seems on the surface to have nothing to do with what is happening to Joseph. So for now, let's continue our following of Joseph's plight in Egypt. Why the Bible itself seems to do the same thing. Read Genesis 37:36 and Genesis 39:1.

You see? We don't learn anything new. We already knew Ishmaelites and Midianites are the same group in this story. We also didn't learn Potiphar was an Egyptian unless we thought the head of Pharaoh's palace guard might not be Egyptian.

It looks for now that chapter 38 can be left unread, and that no damage will be done to our story. So that is what we'll do.

The first new thing we are told is the last thing any of us would have thought! "And the Lord was with Joseph" (Genesis 39:2a).

Excuse me? Say what? Joseph is in exactly the same position you find yourself repeatedly in life. He is oppressed, lonely, suffering, forgotten, ill-treated, without hope, and forsaken by God. Well, isn't he? Don't tell me what you know because you've read the end of the story. Tell me what you'd think if what had happened to Joseph happened to you. You're a slave in Egypt, and your father thinks you're dead.

Today's assignment: What is your biggest problem in life? Same as mine. My biggest problem is me. Your biggest problem is you. How strong is your faith? Mine is incredibly strong when it comes to praying for you. Sometimes it's not so strong when praying for me.

That's lack of faith. The father of the possessed boy asked Jesus for help (Mark 9:24). He cried with tears. "Lord, I believe; help thou mine unbelief." In what areas do you have unbelief?

_____
_____
_____
_____

Pray that God would increase your faith.

Day 16

I know there are Christians who have great faith. I've met Christians who have trusted God in all manner of terrible circumstances. But sold as a slave by your brothers? Dead to your living parents? Working as a slave in a foreign country where you don't know the language?

"And the Lord was with Joseph, and he was a prosperous man."

What? Be careful not to picture Joseph happy and having fun. In fact, the Bible doesn't say Joseph knew the Lord was with him, or that his prosperity brought him peace. My experience is that prosperity often as not brings you bigger problems.

We read in Hebrews 13:5 that the Lord will never leave us or forsake us. I know that intuitively. I just don't act as though I believe it sometimes.

Read Genesis 39:3–6. Joseph's master saw something different about Joseph. He saw that the Lord was with him. He saw that it was the Lord that made all Joseph did to prosper. This guy is an Egyptian! He doesn't know God! He didn't know God existed before meeting Joseph. Isn't it amazing that even worldly people can often recognize God working in our lives more quickly than we can?

I once counselled a man who was in a crisis in life. This person was in such a tailspin; there was little hope of a good outcome. I remember thinking, *This guy is going to commit suicide!* I thought our meeting was a total waste of time. I shared what I thought were appropriate scriptures. I prayed. You know, I went through the motions. I left him in his downward spiral.

Several years went by, I received a letter from him. It said, "I could see God in your life and I knew he could be there for me if I'd trust him. I just didn't want to hear it that day we talked." Later in the letter, he said, "Thank you for saving my life." That man's life is changed. He's my Facebook friend. It had nothing to do with me! It couldn't have. God accomplished something through me. God did that through Joseph to reach Potiphar. I'm not saying Potiphar became a believer. But what he saw in Joseph, God revealed to him. Potiphar makes Joseph the overseer of his household.

Today's assignment: Do you see God working in your life? _____

Where or How?
_____
_____
_____
_____
_____

Is God "with" you? _____
Pray that God will give you eyes to see Him working in your life every day.

Day 17

Potiphar puts Joseph in such control of his household that Potiphar loses track of all he owns (Genesis 39:6). Potiphar is only aware of what is on his plate. Joseph is in charge of the rest.
Read Genesis 39:7–20.
Are you kidding me? This is just going from bad to worse! Have you ever been sold as a slave by your family? Me either. What was my biggest problem again? I'm embarrassed to tell anyone. And now

Joseph is about to inherit a problem that will make being sold as a slave by his brothers seem like a vacation!

Potiphar is a busy man. Or maybe while Joseph is taking care of Potiphar's business, Potiphar is out recreating somewhere. Potiphar's wife needs more to do too. She has time to lie around the house and seduce teenagers. She casts her eyes upon Joseph and says, "Lie with me."

Well, now it isn't hard to figure out how this is going to turn out—a teenage boy with hormones raging, a brother hated by his siblings, "dead" to his father, in a foreign country, in charge of a big house with a beautiful (you just know she was) wicked older woman trying to seduce him. Don't blame me. It's in the Bible. Let's see…I'd have gladly given anyone fifty to one odds, he'd be in bed with her in ten minutes!

Look at verse 8. "But he refuses." What? Is this boy normal? The answer my friend is *no*! Joseph is a type of Christ. It just wouldn't have worked if he had done what, I'm afraid—no, certain—the majority of seventeen-year-old young men would have done.

Joseph refuses her daily. This isn't a one-time temptation. This is constant. Joseph can't get out of the house. She won't leave. "Day by day" (Genesis 39:10).

Today's assignment: In what areas are you tempted? I already know (1 John 2:16). Same as me. So you too are tempted. Maybe this is one of those days where you don't want to write anything. I understand. But want some great news? Read 1 Corinthians 10:13. Escape is available! We just don't look hard enough for it. Maybe we don't want to escape. That's a bigger problem.

Pray. Talk to God right now about this. Remember the Lord's model prayer? "Lead us not into temptation." Lead us in a path that takes us in a godly direction Lord.

Tell God what's on your heart.

Day 18

How many days does Joseph refuse her? We don't know. I'll bet it was lots. Joseph speaks of his responsibility as a worker. He speaks of his loyalty to Potiphar. But look at Genesis 39:9, "How then can I do this great wickedness and sin against God?"

I'll tell you how, Joseph! God forsook you, so who cares? I mean, you should be obedient to God if He blesses you and makes your life a joy—sure! I'd understand that. But to care about sin after God allowed my brothers to sell me as a slave? I don't think so.

Notice too that Joseph didn't say, "How could someone…" or "How could a person…," He makes it personal. "How then can I do this great wickedness and sin against God?"

Joseph has things to do that require his presence in the house. One day, he goes in alone (Genesis 39:11). She is close by, close enough to catch his garment. "Lie with me" for the umpteenth time. He flees, leaving his garment behind (verse 12).

I don't know if Joseph ran out naked or if anyone saw him. It didn't make any difference. Potiphar's wife knew it was never going to happen. She had been scorned by a Hebrew teen. She could never allow the truth to get out.

Think of the hypocrisy and level of sin in this woman. She who coveted, she who begged daily for adultery, she who had no shame, she who cries out! She has been insulted. She has been ill-treated. She has been mocked. She has been attacked! She has been attacked on her own bed by this "Hebrew" that "he" (Potiphar) stupidly brought into their house! She's going to stay pretty close to that garment (verse 16) because it's her only evidence. Potiphar returns and hears the story. He believes his wife. Joseph is falsely accused and taken into custody (Genesis 39:20).

Does any of this sound familiar? (Matthew 26:60).

Today's assignment: Life can go haywire in a heartbeat. The worst thing you are dealing with today can become insignificant tomorrow due to an even bigger problem.

Ever have a circumstance like this?

_____
_____
_____
_____
_____

How did you cope?

_____
_____
_____
_____
_____

Pray God would give you the faith to trust Him when life gets crazy.

Day 19

Read Genesis 39:21.

Give me a break! Never in the history of man to this point was there a human being more obviously forsaken by God than Joseph. I mean think about it. He's done nothing wrong really. Oh, he's a sinner all right. The Bible just doesn't record any. And he's at the bottom now. Why? Because he is precisely where God needs him to be to accomplish God's will on earth. Think Joseph's troubles are over? You fool!

You see, here's the mistake we make. We wrongly assume we have to be problem free, trouble free, and at the pinnacle of a successful life to be effectively used by God…or at least we want that. But look around you. The body of Christ is made up of quadriplegic artists, motivational speakers with MS, legless war survivors tramping for Jesus, Christians from horrible backgrounds whose lives and testimonies are walking paradoxes (2 Corinthians 12:10). Think about your own adversities. I've heard them all. Why do anything for Jesus? Are you just stupid? Don't you know when to quit?

I don't know about you, but I'd like the Lord to show me mercy a different way. No, thank you, I'm going to pass on being sold as a slave to foreigners by my brothers, being falsely accused of rape by my master's wife, being thrown into prison without a trial, and having no hope. Thanks anyway!

Today's assignment: "And the Lord was with Joseph." Really? Do you believe that? Well then, tell me please, why do you sometimes think the Lord isn't with you?

_____
_____
_____
_____
_____

Pray that you will be able to trust God regardless of the circumstances of your life.

Day 20

Read Genesis 39:22–23.

I give up! I really do! Joseph must just be stupid! This is exactly what happened last time! I can predict with 100 percent certainty that this is going to turn out badly. I learn from my lessons in life. If I'm trusting the Lord for protection in some area of my life and circumstances deteriorate, I try to avoid that area. I would never be so dumb as to think when things are going to crap (sorry) that, "and the Lord was with Duke and shewed him mercy." Why if the Lord was doing all that, I wouldn't have any problems, would I? Well, would I? What do you think? How do you react to adversity? I'll bet I know how you react. You think all your troubles come from Satan, don't you? You're wrong.

Listen, a teenage girl dove off a dock. Her head hit the bottom, and she broke her neck. The foolish among us ask, "Where was God?" I'll tell you where God was. "And the Lord was with Joni Erickson." That's where he was! And He showed her mercy. She didn't drown.

And she doesn't even know me, but she has blessed my life with hope and rejoicing. She has given me courage. I'm a former active duty marine. I flew helicopters in Vietnam. I got hit nine times by enemy fire. But I get my strength from the Lord. Thanks to quadriplegics like Joni Erickson. And one day in the kingdom, I'm going to run up to her—no—she's going to run up to me and throw her arms around me and just smile. Joni has yielded her life to the Lord. I want to keep my life most days. She "gets it!" She understands that the Lord was with Joseph in spite of how the circumstances of his life looked.

God uses prostitutes, alcoholics, drug addicts, quadriplegics, blind, deaf, people from diverse sordid backgrounds—all of whom have become Christians—to minister to reach others currently going through those same circumstances.

It wouldn't surprise me if Joseph met a couple of prisoners going through the same anguish he is.

Today's assignment: Are you going through adversity? Can you write about it? Maybe it will help.

_____
_____
_____
_____

And the Lord was with _____
(fill in your name)

Day 21

Read Genesis 40:1–4.

Bingo! Wow! That was fast. I wonder what a butler and a baker could do to kindle Pharaoh's ire enough to get them thrown in the slammer. Notice that Joseph was bound there. So much for God showing him mercy! I guess he did win favor with the keeper of the prison. But hadn't he "won favor" with Potiphar. Oh no, he "found grace" with Potiphar. Maybe his relationship with these two will work out better.

Uh-oh! Dreams! (Genesis 40:5–8. This isn't good. Dreams get Joseph in trouble. All of his problems started with dreams, didn't they?

It's so easy for me not to share what I know about God with people. Remaining silent when I have lots to say is one of my greatest gifts. I am an introvert with a quiet personality. My kids have always said I don't have a personality.

Joseph is not like me. Maybe it's because he is so much like Christ. I don't like that thought very much. But how can Joseph blurt out that dream interpretations belong to God? And if they belong to God, why does Joseph want to hear them?

Wow! These dreams just tell me these two are wacko! But Joseph gave God credit ahead of time. Now I ask you, do you trust God? Every Christian reading this probably says, "Sure!" But do you trust Him to come through for you when you need Him? How about after your siblings sold you as a slave and you get falsely accused of a crime and thrown into prison? All right then, tell me you trust God to come through for you. I know you don't. If the truth were known, you probably don't trust Him even though your life isn't going anywhere nearly as badly as Joseph's.

Today's assignment: It's true, isn't it? Sometimes you don't trust God to come through for you. Why is that? Lack of faith. Want to increase your faith? (Romans 10:17). Read the Bible daily. Are you waiting for a clear answer from God? Name it.

_____
_____
_____

Ask God to use His Word to provide you an answer. Think He'll say, "No?" I don't.

Pray for wisdom to recognize God's answer.

Day 22

Here is a nugget for you. One of those pieces of advice from an old man who's made a lot of mistakes. It can change your weak faith into strength. It's simple! You don't have to be smart to get it. Read this story about Joseph in the Bible and think about it. Think of how Joseph reacts to adversity in life. Think about how it would be quite reasonable and justifiable for him to react. Think of how you would react if Joseph's problems happened to you. If there is a difference, what is God telling you about your faith?

I think we read these stories in the Bible, and we act as though they are just words on a page. We think we are reading a history book at best. We forget God is speaking to us. He's not speaking to us about Joseph either. He's speaking to us about us!

Joseph trusts God not based on the circumstances of his life but in spite of the circumstances of his life. He trusts God because God is God. Do you get that? I don't think you do. I think the sovereignty of God scares you. I think you trust God only if you are relatively free of life's problems.

This story of Joseph's life is an Old Testament type of Christ. You probably see that by now. But Joseph's story is much more than that. It is an instruction for us.

Trust God in spite of your fear He has forsaken you. He hasn't. The lousy circumstances of your life may be part of a plan He has to accomplish something great. Now listen, Joseph is not suffering the consequences of his past sin. But you might be. Circumstances you're suffering, regardless of where they come from though, don't hinder God from blessing you and causing your life to prosper.

Today's assignment: Think about your problems. I've got a good idea what they are. They're like mine. Now think about God. He sent His Son to die in your place! Now He's going to forsake you? That's just plain stupid!

Pray whatever is on your heart. And, oh yeah, Joseph is headed for another disappointment.

Write a note to God about your problems. Write another note about your faith. Then burn them.

I'm serious! Write those notes and then go outside and burn them.

Day 23

Read Genesis 40:9–22.

So the butler dreams he's squeezing grapes, and the baker dreams buzzards are eating off his head. Joseph tells the butler he'll be restored to his former position in three days. He tells the baker he'll be beheaded in three days. Then Joseph tells the butler to please remember him and to speak kindly of him to Pharaoh.

Everything comes to pass exactly the way God revealed it to Joseph. Baker is dead. Butler is released. So far, so good…not that the baker is dead, just that Joseph's interpretations were right.

Now read Genesis 40:23. Let's talk about that. Neither the butler nor the baker probably believed Joseph. But day three comes, and everything happens as he predicted. The butler is out! Okay, follow this with me. Don't just read verses. Think about it. Do you think it is at all possible that the butler simply forgot? Of course you don't! The butler would be telling everyone about Joseph! He'd be telling this story for the rest of his life! And it hadn't just momentarily slipped his mind. He forgets about Joseph for two years! Now unless this butler is suffering from some form of dementia, there is no earthly way he could possibly have forgotten about Joseph! And there is the answer, "no earthly way." It just wasn't time for Joseph to be released. So God "reached down" and blotted any memory of Joseph from the butler's brain. You see, God knew Joseph had two more dreams to interpret.

After two more years in prison, things must have looked bleak for Joseph. I remember a rather difficult day in my life. A girl I had dated for over a year in college had a conversation with me about our future together. I was headed for Vietnam, and she was against the war. It just wasn't going to work out. We said goodbye. The same hour we said goodbye, I met my wife. We had never spoken before.

We have been married fifty-three blissfully happy years. It doesn't take God long to bring about His will in the lives of His people.

Today's assignment: What are you waiting for God to do in your life?

_____
_____
_____
_____
_____

Can you be patient?
Pray God will give you the patience you need.

Day 24

Read Genesis 41:1–8.

Now Pharaoh is dreaming! Seven fat cows eaten by seven skinny cows. Seven succulent ears of corn being eaten by seven sorry ears of corn. He calls Egypt's best magicians. They're stumped.

Read Genesis 41:9–14.

God intervenes. He causes the butler to remember Joseph after being brain-dead for two years. The butler tells Pharaoh about Joseph. Pharaoh says, "Go get him!"

Notice that even though Joseph has confidence the dream will be interpreted; he doesn't take credit for it. What would you have done? I might have "allowed" Pharaoh to think it was my wit that figured out the dreams. I hope not, but I think I might have.

Read Genesis 41:15–24.

Joseph says, "It is not in me: God shall give Pharaoh an answer of peace." How did Joseph know it would be an answer of peace? That part bothers me. What if God said the dreams meant Egypt will be destroyed?

Read Genesis 41:25–32.

When Joseph hears the dreams, God gives him an immediate interpretation. Joseph explains to Pharaoh that God ordained seven years of plenty followed by seven years of famine.

Read Genesis 41:33–36.

Where does this plan come from? How did that stuff about food storage just pop into Joseph's head? Did he know how to store grain for seven years? No, God knew how. And just as God has often placed what men thought were preposterous plans in the minds of men throughout history, He places a thought in Joseph's mind.

I have to laugh when I think about Joseph's personality. He dreams a dream where he is lord over his family, and he shares it. He hears two inmates discussing dreams, and he intervenes. Pharaoh has a dream, and Joseph blurts out what it means. Now he's telling Pharaoh how to run Egypt for the next fourteen years! Wonder how this is going to turn out.

Today's assignment: Could you counsel someone? Could you tell them how God works in the lives of men? All of those kinds of helps for people are in the Bible. Counselling books are available at Christian bookstores. Are you gifted that way?

_____
_____
_____
_____
_____

Pray God would equip you to speak to others who are without hope.

Day 25

All I can say is if I had been in Joseph's place, things would have turned out differently. I can keep a secret forever. I wouldn't have told my family about my dream. I never would have talked to two strangers in prison about their dreams. If I'd been in prison for eleven years in a foreign country, I wouldn't have been talking to anyone! Talk to strangers about why they look so sad? (Genesis 40:6–7). Not likely! So I'd have never gotten an audience with Pharaoh. You see, I don't talk to people. Well, usually. God has to shout at me to get me to talk to people, and even then, I'm a little scared.

The body of Christ is made up of people with different talents and personalities. God uses us all. Or at least He can use us all if we let Him. God has Joseph precisely where He needs him! Something great is about to happen!

Read Genesis 41:37–41.

Having a bold witness allows the world to see God working in your life. Joseph said, "God shall give Pharaoh." He didn't say, "Maybe you could ask God what the dream means. Who knows. Maybe he'll answer you. I ask Him for stuff, and sometimes He answers me. Although I've been praying to get out of prison now for thirteen years, and it hasn't helped much." No, Joseph speaks boldly. God's power doesn't depend on circumstances. It doesn't even depend on physics! It depends on faith!

Pharaoh thinks Joseph's idea is a good one. So do his sycophantic servants. Pharaoh can also tell "the spirit of God" is in Joseph. Hey, it says so right there in verse 38!

Could someone tell that the spirit of God is in you? Or might they say, "He is? Could have fooled me!"

Pharaoh goes on to say that he understands that God is the one who has shown Joseph all this. So he puts Joseph in charge of all Egypt (Verse 41).

Today's assignment: Are you a bold witness for Christ or are you more like me and don't care to talk to people?

_____
_____
_____
_____
_____

How are you gifted spiritually?

_____
_____
_____
_____

Pray that God would give you the boldness necessary to use your spiritual gifts to minister to others.

Day 26

Read Genesis 41:42–46.

Pharaoh puts a ring, not just any ring, Pharaoh's own ring on Joseph's hand. Joseph is arrayed in gold and fine clothes and riding a chariot. I don't know how happy God was about the horses (Deuteronomy 17:16). He may not have been thrilled about the Egyptian wife either. I just know He didn't like the new name! Zaphnath-Paaneah? Who would?

Joseph is thirty. He had been sold as a slave thirteen years ago (Genesis 41:46). Eleven years in prison till he met the butler and baker, two more waiting for Pharaoh to dream. He is now ready to start the "ministry" God has for him on this earth. His age is no coincidence. "And Jesus himself began to be about thirty years of age" (Luke 3:23). Jesus was thirty when He started His earthly ministry.

What is Joseph's real connection to Christ? We see the many ways he is an Old Testament type of Christ. But is there some more direct connection? Does it have anything to do with what is happening now?

Now Joseph Goes "out from the presence of Pharaoh and went throughout all the land of Egypt." From prison to complete freedom, and not just freedom, he's in charge! I know where I'd have gone first—to Potiphar's house and put his wife in prison for thirteen years. Then I would have had a stern conversation with that butler who forgot me for two years.

Read Genesis 41:47–53.

Joseph is now thirty-seven years old. His Egyptian wife bore him two sons during the seven years of plenty. First Manasseh and then Ephraim. Joseph has forgotten all his "toil and his father's house." Twenty years have gone by since Joseph was separated from his family. If you are thirty-seven years old or older, think of your life the first seventeen years, and then consider what happened in the twenty years after that. Did those years change you?

Joseph is changed. Joseph looks Egyptian, speaks Egyptian, and for all practical purposes, he *is* Egyptian.

Today's assignment: Can God turn your sorrow to joy?

_____
_____
_____
_____
_____

Do you think He will?

_____
_____
_____
_____
_____

Read John 16:19–22.
Pray for God to turn your sorrow to joy even now in this life.

Day 27

Read Genesis 41:53–57.

Bad times are ahead for anyone outside of Egypt. The famine was in all lands (verse 54). But Joseph, with lots of help from God, had done it! There was bread in Egypt. It was going to cost you though. Joseph is selling it not only to Egyptians but to people of all nations that come to Egypt for food. This had been no small feat. It was nothing short of a miracle! The miracle had been performed by

God. God had foreknowledge of the famine. He resists direct intervention in natural disasters and how they affect the affairs of men. But God was with Joseph every step of the way to Dothan, every step of the way to Egypt, every step in prison, every step of the seven years of plenty, and now during the early part of the famine.

There is bread in Egypt for one reason. God did it. And He didn't do it so Egyptians could get fat. He didn't do it so Pharaoh could get rich.

Well, then what is the reason? Bet you can't guess.

Today's assignment: Is there purpose in natural disasters? Don't be afraid to answer "I don't know." What do you really think?

_____
_____
_____
_____
_____

Isn't it frustrating when some nonbeliever asks you, "How can there be a God if…blah, blah, blah, blah, blah! What do you say?

_____
_____
_____
_____
_____

Pray this study will give you an answer that makes those people think!

Day 28

Read Genesis 42:1–4.

Jacob is with his sons and their families back in what would one day become Israel. The famine was affecting his family to the point of death (verse 2). The word of food being available in Egypt had spread to all affected countries. He tells his sons to quit standing around, looking at each other and get down (south) to Egypt to buy food and keep the family alive. The ten oldest brothers go. But once again, Jacob has a favorite.

Movies I've seen have always depicted Benjamin as a young boy at this stage of the story. He wasn't. He was about thirty-five. He may have looked young, but he was married and had ten sons! Benjamin was a man quite capable of making the trip with his brothers. Jacob is doing the same thing with Benjamin that he had done with Joseph. Joseph and Benjamin are the only two sons of Rachel. Rachel died during Benjamin's birth. She had named him Benoni (son of my sorrow). Jacob renamed him Benjamin (son of my right hand). I imagine Benjamin's brothers are jealous of him and resented his special treatment.

Read Genesis 42:5.

Joseph is at least thirty-seven years old now. He was seventeen when he went to prison, thirteen years in prison, seven years of plenty _____, thirty-seven years old.

Reuben is near fifty now. Joseph's brothers have probably never left Canaan before. The sixty-three mile grazing trip to Dothan may have been the furthest they had ever ventured from home I guess. This trip to Egypt is about 230 miles. It probably took seven to ten days one way. They travel south, then west across the northern Sinai Peninsula on their way to the country into which they had sold their brother. What did they think about on the way? Was Joseph possibly alive? Certainly not. But if he was, where was he? What was his life like after he left them? Could God forgive them? This was a horrible trip with no one talking. You just know it was.

Today's assignment: Do you remember your sins? Of course you do. We all do. It's a wonder we can smile. Do you really think God forgets your sin? Write what you think about that.

_____
_____
_____
_____
_____

Read Psalm 103:12. How far is that exactly?

Pray for the faith to believe forgiveness is really possible for you.

Day 29

Read Genesis 42:6–9.

Joseph hadn't seen his brothers in twenty years, nor of course, had they seen him. Being older than Joseph at the time they sold him into slavery and still looking very Jewish, they hadn't changed in appearance nearly as much as Joseph had. He, on the other hand, had changed greatly. Their seventeen-year-old brother was now closer to thirty-eight. He was a man, not just any man mind you. But this Zaphnath-paaneah was the governor of Egypt! He wore Egyptian makeup and clothing. He spoke Egyptian.

Joseph sees his brothers bowing to him on the floor, and he remembers his dream of this scene he'd had more than twenty years ago. He accuses them of being spies. They insist they are not.

How things have changed for Joseph! He is highly revered by the lowliest slaves all the way to Pharaoh himself. He has become the hero of Egypt! His wisdom comes from God and even Pharaoh acknowledges that. Unfortunately for Pharaoh, admitting God is with someone doesn't make you a believer. But Joseph is a believer.

Read Genesis 42:10–17.

His brothers avoid eye contact with him. They humble themselves as best they can by kneeling with their faces to the floor. You know they had to be thinking they'd have rather starved than be on this trip!

Joseph was thinking far differently. He remembered his dream about sheaves. "We were binding sheaves in the field, and lo, my sheaf arose, and also stood upright, and behold, your sheaves stood round about and made obeisance to my sheaf" (Genesis 37:6–8). It had come true!

Now he speaks. "Where are you from?" They answer meekly. Joseph says, "No! You are spies!" They say, "We've only come to buy food." They describe their family with a minor reference to Joseph. Joseph knows they speak the truth, but he must ensure he doesn't lose contact with them. He can do anything he pleases. He needs authorization from no one. He informs them that nine of them must stay in Egypt as prisoners while one returns to Canaan to fetch Benjamin. Then he puts all ten of them in prison for three days. Three days! He had been in prison thirteen years!

Today's assignment: Joseph's brothers are bowing down to him just as their sheaves had bowed to his in his dream more than twenty years ago. So his dream was prophetic. There is much prophecy in scripture. If God said it, do you believe it will come true?

_____
_____
_____
_____

God has given prophecies about Israel, Russia, Libya, Ethiopia, Persia, other countries, Christians, lost people. Do you know what they are?

_____

Do you think you should know?

_____

Pray God would replace some waste of time currently in your life with a curiosity for prophecy. He will.

Day 30

Read Genesis 42:18–20.
Joseph says, What? "I fear God? Which God?" We know. But what did his brothers think? "This do and live." They're thinking, *Yes, we'll do anything!* Joseph says, "Let one of your brethren be bound in the house of your prison: go ye, carry corn for the famine of your house: But…" (Uh-oh, here it comes), "but bring your youngest

brother to me: so shall your worth be verified and ye shall not die." And they did so.

Read Genesis 42:21–23.

They now discuss their guilt concerning Joseph. They assume they are now suffering because of their sin. And they're right! But God isn't punishing them. Joseph is! They are openly discussing what they had done to Joseph right in front of him. Well, in front of Zaphnath-paaneah. But he's Egyptian. He can't understand them… or so they think.

Today's assignment: If our sins are forgiven and God remembers them no more, why is it we sometimes suffer because of them?

_____
_____
_____
_____
_____

What consequences have you suffered?

_____
_____
_____
_____
_____

Pray that God would minimize the effects of those consequences.

Day 31

Read Genesis 42:24.

Joseph has to leave them. He wept (John 11:35). Reuben, the weak leader, says something like, "I told you so." in verse 22. When he had left while Joseph was in the pit, it left the next oldest in charge. Who was that? (Genesis 29:33).

Joseph returns to them and took Simeon. He binds Simeon, the one who was in charge when Joseph was sold as a slave. He binds him right in front of their eyes. He wants them to remember.

Be careful not to think Joseph is committing a sin that I have overlooked. He hasn't lied. He is testing his brothers to determine their character. In the three days, they were imprisoned. Joseph devised a plan to save his family from the famine and assure himself he would not lose contact with them.

And now look what he orders! Read Genesis 42:25–28. He instructs his servants to fill their sacks with corn, food for their journey, and give them back their money! I have to laugh at their reaction when they discover their brother's money. Their hearts failed them! "What is this that God hath done unto us?" (Genesis 42:28).

Today's assignment: What kind of ruler would you be? Seriously, might you be vindictive? Just a little maybe? Who would you get even with? Would you do worse to them than they had done to you? What if you could get away with anything and suffer no consequences? Joseph could. What would you do?

_____

_____

_____

_____

_____

I'd be my enemies' worst nightmare!

Pray, pray what you need to pray here. I'm praying God never allows me to have the kind of power Joseph had.

Day 32

Read Genesis 42:29–36.

After nearly a month, they return to their father. They tell him everything that happened. They refer to Joseph as "the man who is the Lord of the land." I don't know how broken up Jacob was over Simeon being in prison in Egypt. He refers to Simeon with identical verbiage as Joseph. He believes Joseph was dead. Did he think Simeon would die in prison? (verse 36).

There is one thing of which I am certain. The worst news that Jacob heard was that Benjamin had to go to Egypt with his older brothers or Simeon would never get out of prison. I don't think his concern was for Simeon but rather what might befall his favorite, Benjamin.

Read Genesis 42:37–38.

What's this? Reuben? The one who was in charge when his brothers sold Joseph behind his back? "Slay my two sons if I bring him (Benjamin) not to thee" (Genesis 42:37). Think about that. I wouldn't allow Reuben to be in charge of a three-legged dog! How on earth would it minimize Jacob's grief over the loss of his favorite son to have to turn around and kill two of his grandsons? That is the craziest plan in the Bible since Adam ate the forbidden fruit!

Now Jacob doesn't have to think about this plan of Reuben's very long. He can stop the death of his favorite son, Benjamin, and avoid having to kill his grandsons with a plan of his own. At least he thinks he can. How about "my son (Benjamin) shall not go down with you." End of story (verse 38).

I'll bet Jacob started praying harder for the famine to be over. The problem was it was far from over. You see, here is what is going on. Jacob is devising his way, but God was directing his steps. (Proverbs 16:9).

Today's assignment: Is what you are doing today part of the plan you had for yourself ten years ago? _____ Five years ago?_____ One year ago?_____ What events happened in your life that resulted in you being where you are today?

_____
_____
_____
_____

Do you think it's possible that God directed your steps to get you here?

_____

What are you willing to risk to have your own way? Jacob was willing to put his whole family at risk in order to keep Benjamin safe. How about you?

_____
_____
_____
_____

Pray that the Lord will make His steps for you obvious. Then pray for courage to follow those steps.

Day 33

Read Genesis 43:1–10.

Jacob is getting old. He forgets things. After all, he is 130 (Genesis 47:28). Judah speaks softly to his father. Jacob had already stated that Benjamin would not be going to Egypt.

Notice finally, Reuben has been relieved of command. He gives no further orders to his brothers in this story. This should have happened long ago. Jacob needs advice on parenting.

Simeon is in prison. He was the next oldest. Then came Levi. I don't know where he is. Levi is older than Judah, but he and Simeon had murdered a whole city of innocent men (Genesis 34:25). Maybe he wasn't fit for command either.

Judah speaks sensibly. "Send Benjamin with me that we may all live…I will be surety for him." Jacob listens and finally assents.

From this point on in the story, Judah is a changed man. He has had more than twenty years to think about his plan to sell Joseph into slavery. Let's see how different he really is.

Today's assignment:
Can a person change?

Can you give a person a second chance?

Have you ever?

Do you know anyone who deserves a second chance now?

Pray God will give you a forgiving spirit. Also—pray God would bring about changes in you that are necessary.

Day 34

Read Genesis 43:11–14.

Jacob relents. But he insists on doing everything he can to bring about a good result. Here is the plan: "Take lots of stuff. Take stuff that's even too nice for us to use except on special occasions. Also, take double money, plus the money you all found in your sacks. And take my most precious thing—take Rachel's son Benjamin. And I pray to God you all get to come home. But I have little confidence I'll ever see you again." That quote is all my paraphrase.

Read Genesis 43:15.

Off go ten brothers to Egypt. Judah is in charge. Judah is responsible for the success of the mission. He is responsible for Benjamin's safety.

Remember, Reuben is no longer in charge. Reuben's last words were that ridiculous suggestion that Jacob should kill Reuben's two sons if Reuben should fail to bring Benjamin back from Egypt. Let's see, how does this work? Reuben fails (again), and his two sons pay with their lives! Thanks, Dad. If Reuben says anything else in his life, God didn't think it was important enough to record in the Bible.

The ten brothers arrive in Egypt. They stand before Joseph. Well, they think they're standing before Zaphnath-paaneah, the governor of Egypt. They are frightened. They are tired. They wonder how this man who had them all thrown in prison the last time they were in Egypt will treat them this time.

Today's assignment: Just because the Bible doesn't say any family members were praying doesn't mean they weren't. Do you think Jacob was praying? I do. How about Reuben? Judah? Benjamin? What about Joseph?

_____

Do you pray?

_____

When? _____ Just shorter prayers during the day? Or do you have a regular prayer time?

_____

Pray your prayer life would improve. But when it does, get ready to see Satan in action! He isn't going to like it. Whatever time you pick, Satan will attack. Don't give him the victory.

Day 35

Read Genesis 43:16–23.
Well, the brothers are now standing before Joseph. If Simeon can see through the bars, he's straining his neck to see if Benjamin is with them.
Joseph sees Benjamin. He instructs his servants to take his brothers to his home and prepare a feast.
His brothers are about to pass out. They are afraid. They think they are about to be made slaves because of the mix-up about the money when they were last here. They confess to Joseph's chief steward the entire account of finding their money in their sacks when they stopped at an inn on their way home.

Look at what Joseph's steward says to them! "Fear not. Your God and the God of your father, hath given you treasure in your sacks." Think they were a little surprised? And Simeon is released!

Read Genesis 43:24–34.

As soon as they are inside, they wash, their donkeys are fed, and the brothers get water. They bring the present inside that they had brought for Joseph. When he comes in, they bow to the earth before him.

Joseph asks, "Is your father well, the old man of whom you spake? Is he yet alive?" They answer, "Thy servant our father is in good health, he is yet alive." And they bowed before him again to the earth.

Now Joseph sees Benjamin. "Is this your younger brother of whom ye spake unto me?" And Joseph says, "God be gracious unto thee my son." Joseph is overcome. He retires to his own chamber and weeps. He refreshes himself and returns. The twelve brothers eat together and notice that Benjamin receives the best and the most food. They were all merry. Could life get any better?

Today's assignment: Don't you find it curious that Joseph's steward seems to know about the God of the Jews? If you were in prison in a foreign country, would anyone have learned about Jesus? How about if you became governor of the land? Joseph, the Hebrew, speaks Egyptian to his brothers through an interpreter. It seems Joseph's steward, the Egyptian, speaks Hebrew to them. Who taught him Hebrew? How does he know about their God? Would you witness to others if you were in a situation like Joseph?

_____
_____
_____
_____
_____

When things are going well in your life, do you think it's because God is with you then?

_____
_____
_____
_____

When things are going badly in your life, do you think it's because God isn't with you?

_____
_____
_____
_____

Pray that God would give you boldness to witness about him in every situation.

Day 36

Read Genesis 44:1–3.

Oh sure, verse 1 starts out nice. But I was waiting for this. Revenge! It's what most of us might have done. Accuse them of something they didn't do and then throw them in prison. Hard not to smile.

But wait! Is that what Joseph is doing? Or is this a test? Joseph was hated by his brothers because of his special treatment by Jacob. They were jealous. They wanted to kill him but ended up selling him as a slave. Would they be just as happy now to rid themselves of Daddy's new favorite, Benjamin? Joseph wanted to find out whether his brothers had changed.

Joseph commanded. Think about that. How differently things turned out compared to what Joseph's brothers had intended when they sold him. Think of the utterly miserable lives these men had lived the last twenty-two years. Every stranger that approached their homes in Hebron might have been Joseph returning. Twenty-two years of worry. Did they have a plan? Would they kill him? Would they leave Canaan? Think of their misery.

But today is the happiest day of their lives.

Joseph commanded that his silver cup be placed in Benjamin's sack. It was done.

I want to tell you something about life. I'm old. It's kind of fun being old. You can say anything you want. So here it is. Your blissfully happy life can become a nightmare in a moment. I have a friend. He was living one of the happiest days of his life. The phone rang. He learned his oldest son had plummeted off a mountain in a convertible with three other boys. My friend's son was in the hospital. My friend started to pack to travel to the state where the accident had happened. The phone rang again. My friend's son had died. Two years after the accident, my friend told me that the second phone call split time in half. He said, "There was my life before that phone call. And there was my life after that phone call." He said it was as though two different people lived those two lives.

There is a verse of scripture I'm sure many people have read and not understood. Solomon wrote it. "And if the tree fall toward the south, or toward the north, in the place where the tree falleth, there it shall be" (Ecclesiastes 11:3b). Some things are final. When they happen, there is no undoing them. Some happen as circumstances over which you have no control. Some are done to you by others. Some you bring on yourself. But when they happen, they are final.

Joseph's brothers are about to experience one of those time-splitting moments. On the happiest day of their lives, they are about to live through their worst nightmare.

It's their happiest day because this Zaphnath-paaneah, whom they greatly feared, treated them to lunch, let Simeon out of prison, gave them food to take back to Canaan, and Benjamin was safe! They were all laughing and joking as they travelled homeward. Judah must have been ecstatic.

Today's assignment: Have you ever had one of those time splitting moments? What was it?

_____
_____
_____
_____

What did you learn through it?

_____
_____
_____
_____

Have you ever brought on problems in your own life due to your own sin?

_____
_____
_____
_____

Pray. I know that some sins can cause consequences that never seem to go away. Pray that God will minimize consequences of sins you've committed for which you have already been forgiven.

Day 37

Read Genesis 44:4–13.

Yes, Judah is reveling in his success. I'm sure he can't wait to get home and have Dad laughing and patting him on the back.

But just outside the city, Judah's joy turns to fright! This is the steward of Zaphnath-paaneah! Why does he look so stern? What is this he is saying? Rewarded evil for good? Us? Never?

Think back twenty-two years, men. What had Joseph done? He did what his father had asked. And what was that? To check on your well-being. Was that good or evil? Good, you say? How did you reward him? With evil? So then, you rewarded evil for good, just like the steward is saying. Right? Oh, I see. That was then. This time you're innocent.

The steward searches for the "stolen" cup. He makes them sweat. He starts with the oldest. He searches Reuben, Simeon, Levi, Judah, Dan, Naphtali, Gad, Asher, Issachar, Zebulun, and finally, Benjamin. But the older brothers aren't worried. Benjamin would *never* steal something.

What? He did steal it apparently. Are you kidding me? They ripped their clothes! They repack and head back to the home of the ruler.

They know they face either death or life as slaves. What could be worse? How about being set free and having to return home and tell Jacob that Benjamin is in prison for life? Yeah, that would be worse!

"Be sure your sin will find you out" (Numbers 32:23b). Too bad that hadn't been written yet. The guy who wrote it (Moses) wasn't yet born.

Today's assignment: So just like that—your joy can turn to sorrow in an instant! Do you think God comes and goes in your life? Be honest.

_____
_____
_____
_____
_____

What makes Him come? When you're good?

_____
_____
_____
_____

What makes Him leave? When you're bad?

_____
_____
_____
_____

Do you think you're right about all this?

_____

Pray God would reveal His presence in your life to you in good and bad times. Because He's there! He really is!

Day 38

Read Genesis 44:14–15.

These guys spend more time with their faces on the ground than in any other position with this ruler. I have to laugh. Oh, I get it. Joseph's dream came true in threes (Genesis 42:6, 43:26, 44:14).

Read Genesis 44:16–17.

Finally, Judah confesses! I know he left out a lot of details, but he's scared to death, and this important man doesn't have time for details. If Judah only knew the truth. Judah volunteers to be a slave for life. Zaphnath-paaneah says, "No thanks. You can go free. But I'm keeping Benjamin."

Judah's worst fear has come to pass. The thing he had feared most on the long trip to Egypt with Benjamin was happening. But he, at least, was safe. Would he simply go home without Benjamin and lie about what had happened as he had concerning Joseph? What kind of man had Judah become in twenty-two years? That's what Joseph wants to know.

Read Genesis 44:18–32.

Judah is allowed to tell about Jacob, Joseph, and Benjamin. He explains that Jacob has much love for Benjamin, and that returning to Canaan without Benjamin will result in Jacob dying of grief. Judah at last explains that he "became surety for the lad unto my father, saying if I bring him not unto thee, then I shall bear the blame to my father forever" (verse 32).

Read Genesis 44:33–34.

Here is one of the most beautiful verses of scripture in God's word. "Now therefore, I pray thee, let thy servant (me, Judah) abide instead of the lad a bondman (slave) to my lord (Zaphnath-paaneah); and let the lad (Benjamin) go up (north, home) with his brethren" (verse 33).

That's how you do it, Reuben! Are you listening? That's leadership! That's self-sacrifice! That's interceding on someone's behalf. And Reuben's sons don't need to be killed by their grandfather.

Today's assignment: Protecting yourself doesn't have to be taught. It comes naturally. Being willing to "take one for the team," you know, going up to bat when you *know* you're going to be thrown at, needs to be taught. Judah changed in twenty-two years. He was willing to "take one for the team." Are you?

_____
_____
_____
_____
_____

In the marine corps, we were actually trained to jump on a live grenade. (Well, they were dummies.) But we all got the message. The grenade would probably kill you anyway. But if it didn't, I can assure you you'd wish you'd jumped on it.

Pray God would give you the courage to do the right things.

Day 39

Read Genesis 45:1–4.

Joseph cannot bear to hear more. He orders all Egyptians out of the room. He cries. Judah has been transformed during these twenty-two years. He is no longer the jealous, hateful, greedy brother who had Joseph sold as a slave. Remember, the last words Joseph had heard Judah speak were, "What profit is it if we slay our brother and conceal his blood? Come let us sell him." Today, Judah offered himself as a slave. Joseph may wonder why the fourth oldest brother is in charge, but if he does, he doesn't say so.

Joseph is crying so loudly, the Egyptians heard. The Egyptians in the house of Pharaoh heard. Zaphnath-paaneah, this powerful ruler of Egypt, was crying. And now he speaks…for the first time with his brothers in Hebrew.

"I am Joseph. Doth my father yet live?" And of course, his brothers couldn't answer him. The KJV says, "For they were troubled at his presence." Gotta love that! I'll bet they were troubled!

He orders them nearer. They gather around him. "I am Joseph your brother, whom ye sold into Egypt."

Surely not! That's what the brothers had to be thinking. Then it had to hit them. Their darkest sin was known by this Egyptian ruler. And the Egyptian ruler was Joseph. My head hurts. I'm certain their heads hurt! What is he going to do with them…or rather to them?

Today's assignment: What sin have you committed? Who did you think you sinned against?

_____
_____
_____
_____
_____

You didn't just sin against a person. You sinned against the ruler of the universe! You sinned against one who makes sinning against Zaphnath-paaneah seem funny. What is he going to do to you?

_____

What do you deserve?

_____

What did Joseph's brothers deserve?

_____

Pray right now and thank God for having Jesus pay the penalty for your sin.

Day 40

Read Genesis 45:5.

This is one of the most profound declarations ever uttered by a man. It reveals a heart with a deep faith, a heart with complete trust in God. The one man, who above all other men of the Bible looks the most forsaken by God, declares that it is God who has ordered his steps! While facing those who had sold him as a slave and caused him to be in prison in Egypt from the age of seventeen until thirty and become separated from his family for these past twenty-two years, he implores, "Now then you will all die!" No! "Now, therefore, you will all go to prison!" No! "Now, therefore, you will all be my slaves!" No! But "now, therefore, be not grieved, nor angry with yourselves, that ye sold me hither."

What? No revenge? No punishment? I don't know if I like this.

What does this remind you of? Who is the character of Joseph a picture of? That's right! Jesus! What did Jesus say on the cross when He could have wiped out the Jewish priesthood and the Roman occupiers? "Father, forgive them for they know not what they do" (Luke 23:34).

Then Joseph continues, "For God did send me before you to preserve life."

Stop right there! Whose life? It's true. God did send Joseph to Egypt to preserve life. But Joseph doesn't have a clue whose life God was preserving! The life being preserved is someone you've never heard of in this story.

Bet you can't wait!

Today's assignment: Do you trust God? _____

Do you trust him when things go wrong in your life as much as when they go well?

_____
_____
_____
_____

Pray for the wisdom to understand that when trouble comes to your life, God is just as close to you as always.

Day 41

Are you excited? You should be. This neglected chapter of the Bible is going to get us closer to what God wants every Christian to realize. It will get you closer, just not all the way there. But be patient. God wants you to have a complete understanding about life.

Chapter 38 in Genesis has been treated like a rude parenthetical insertion in what readers have thought was the story of Joseph's life for much of the history of Christianity. Since the Bible was made available to the common man, this chapter has been ignored as if it is a misplaced mistake. Many presentations of "the Coat of Many Colors" or "Joseph in Egypt" leave it out altogether.

After all, it is positively an absolute embarrassment! You have the Lord slaying people, the head of the tribe from which the Messiah would eventually come paying for a prostitute, a man disobeying God in order to protect his financial inheritance, a woman pretending to be a whore and becoming pregnant by her father-in-law. Is that enough?

I've lived long. I have never heard Genesis 38 preached from the pulpit. Pastors seem hard-pressed to find any redeeming value in it. No wonder it has been left out of what looks on the surface like a story about Joseph.

I'm afraid I'm going to have to ask you to sit down. Are you? Good.

The story isn't about Joseph.

In the book of Genesis, from the time Joseph is given the coat of many colors until he reveals his identity to his brothers, the most significant piece of information is found in chapter 38! This same chapter that has been left out of so many accounts of "Joseph's story" is almost the whole story!

Today's Assignment: What do you think the Bible is?
_____
_____
_____
_____
_____

Pray that God will reveal to you, once and for all, what He wants you to "get" from His Word.

Day 42

Read Genesis 38:1–5.

I am so tempted to just stop and let you figure it out for yourself. It took me years of Bible study to finally "get it." I never read what I'm about to reveal to you from any author. I simply got it because I refused to believe God would place something in His Word that could be ignored. Maybe you already know. Maybe I'm just slow.

First of all, let me reassure those of you who think God might have made a mistake inspiring Moses to stick an unrelated chapter in a story about Joseph—He didn't.

Let's look at it and see how it is connected.

"And it came to pass at that time." Stop. At what time? Don't just assume you know. You have to read scripture and compare scripture with scripture to answer this question. From examining other scripture, we discover that the events in chapter 38, and other events closely related to chapter 38, span approximately forty-nine years, give or take a couple. We'll cover that in detail later. We know Joseph had been in Egypt for only twenty-two years by the time he revealed himself to his brothers. All of the events of chapter 38 took place before Joseph had been in Egypt very long. We'll cover that in detail later too. But it is important for you to understand something. The significant thing in chapter 38 takes place close to the time Joseph was sold as a slave. That is why Genesis 37:36 and Genesis 39:1 are almost identical.

So Judah leaves home and travels to Adullam. Adullam was a town southwest of Jerusalem about midway to Lachish in the direction of Gaza on the coast of the Mediterranean Sea. Judah stays with a man named Hirah. Judah then meets the daughter (we never learn her name) of a man named Shuah, and he marries her. She soon has a son named Er. She has two more sons, Onan and Shelah. At the birth of her third son, they are living in Chezib which is believed to be the same as Achzib which was a town in Ashur years later. They are living north of Mount Carmel on the coast of the Mediterranean. I have no idea why.

Today's assignment: Where has life taken you?

_____
_____
_____
_____

My wife, Candy, was born in Manhattan very near the Empire State Building. She now lives here on a farm with me in South Georgia in a place called the Pine Hill Community. She has lived with me in many strange sounding places…Rye, the Blue Ridge Mountains, San Clemente, Okeechobee, you get the idea. That's what life does. All of this takes time. Chapter 38 takes time…you'll see.

Remember we plan our way, but God directs our steps (Proverbs 16:9). That's what happens in life. And life takes time. Several years ago, you may have never heard of the place where you now live. How did you get there? The same way Joseph got to Egypt. The same way Judah got to Chezib.

Pray for patience as God directs your steps through life. You're going to need it.

Day 43

Read Genesis 38:6–11.

This is going to be painful. Judah takes a Canaanite woman as a wife for his oldest son, Er. Verse 2 said Judah took his own wife. Now he didn't just take them like kidnap them or something. He approved of them. Er's wife's name was Tamar.

Verse 7 is downright scary. I suggest you get on your knees right now and thank God you live during the Age of Grace! I have no idea what Er did or how God killed him. Er must have been really bad though because God didn't do that to people very often.

Judah speaks to his second son, Onan, who is also of marrying age (twenty?). Judah tells him to father a child with his older brother's widow in order to raise up a son for his dead brother. This was the first hint of the "kinsman redeemer" provision in Leviticus 25 and Ruth 4. The child would belong to Er not Onan. If Onan did this, the son (if the child was indeed a son, which was Judah's hope) would be an heir to Judah's wealth. That son would receive the greater inheritance of Judah's three sons. Onan would get less than he now stood to get. Onan thinks about this and decides it would be best to ignore what Dad said and not get Tamar pregnant. Onan wasn't quite so convicted that he didn't want to have sexual relations with Tamar—only that he didn't want her to get pregnant. I guess we can classify Onan as "partially convicted." So did God. God slew Onan too. Judah tells Tamar to go home to her own father and live there until Shelah (Judah's youngest son) was old enough to marry—or at least raise up seed for his oldest brother.

We don't know how long it would be until Shelah was old enough to do what Judah promised Tamar. My guess is that it was some single digit number of years. But that's just a guess.

Tamar goes home to her father's house.

Today's assignment: Are you only partially convicted about some sins? When a person gets saved later in life (after adulthood), they often bring with them, certain worldly habits that are sinful. The Holy Spirit begins convicting that person of behaviors which are an impediment to spiritual growth. And the struggle begins—sanctification.

Are you wrestling with the Holy Spirit over such behaviors now?

_____
_____
_____
_____
_____.

Don't leave your answer where anyone can find it.

Pray for conviction first, for eyes to see the way of escape the Lord provides you and the wisdom to go through the door that leads you away from sin.

Day 44

Read Genesis 38:12–16a.

Judah's wife dies. Judah takes a trip to have his sheep sheared. That's why you have sheep. You sell their wool. It seems he may once again be living near Hebron as he went up to Timnath which is northwest of Hebron. Of course, he could also still be living on the coast in which case everything inland would be up.

Someone told Judah's daughter-in-law that he was traveling to Timnath. She immediately dresses herself as a prostitute (which included a veil to cover her face) and goes to a place on the way to Timnath that she knows Judah must pass by. She did this because she saw that Shelah was now fully grown, and she had not been given unto him to marry. Judah had reneged on his promise to Tamar.

In verse 15, Judah sees her and tries to purchase her services. They discuss payment.

Now I want to explain poor Tamar's plight. She is frustrated! She got married, and her husband died. His brother was supposed to give her a son, but he also died. She was told to wait for the youngest brother, but it was now obvious that she wouldn't be allowed to marry him either. So Tamar has no children (especially sons), and she's getting concerned about her future. There will be no one to take care of her in her old age. Don't be too upset with Tamar. That's just the way things were back then.

Tamar is tricking her father-in-law because he didn't keep his promise to have Shelah marry her.

Judah falls for it and desires to have sexual relations with a woman he does not realize is his daughter-in-law.

Today's assignment: Let's talk about keeping your word. It's important. Go back on your word just a couple of times, and you earn a reputation it's difficult to live down. The reason it's difficult is because no one will give you a chance.

Have you given your word and not kept it?

_____
_____
_____
_____
_____

Fix it! Apologize. Keep your promises. You're a Christian. Enough people will be trying to destroy your reputation. Don't help them.

Pray God will remind you to keep your promises and give you the wisdom not to make too many.

Day 45

Read Genesis 38:16b–23.

Back to the payment. Tamar asks, "What wilt thou give me, that thou mayest come in unto me?" She means have sexual relations. Judah doesn't have any money. He hasn't taken his sheep to be shorn yet. So he says, "I will send thee a kid from the flock." Remember, he's taking his sheep to be shorn. He's selling their wool. He says he'll send her one of the kids after he returns home.

Now Tamar doesn't want a kid from the flock any more than you do! So she tells Judah she wants something to hold as security till she gets the kid. Judah asks, "What do you want as security?"

I feel as though I have to interject here. Sometimes we want things (we shouldn't have) so badly that we don't consider consequences. We lose all sense of logic. Judah is about to really mess up here.

Tamar answers, "Please give me everything you have on you that will allow me to positively identify you as the father in a future paternity suit." Well, she doesn't say those exact words, but that's what she means.

Judah says okay. And he "sleeps" with her. Later, he sends the kid as payment, but, of course, the prostitute is nowhere to be found. She never wanted the kid. She didn't want Judah's ring, bracelets, and staff—the security items either. Tamar wanted a son and security only a son could provide her into her old age.

Today's assignment: Think about momentary pleasures in life and the sorrow they can bring. Most pleasures last only moments. Their consequences usually last much longer. Are you suffering any now?

_____
_____
_____
_____
_____

Have you ever suffered consequences of life's "pleasures" in the past?

Pray the Holy Spirit would speak loudly to you about lusts of the flesh.

Day 46

Read Genesis 38:24–30.

It isn't long until Judah learns that his daughter-in-law has "played the harlot and also, behold, she is with child by whoredom."

Judah says, "No problem. Bring her forth and we'll burn her to death."

Some men build a big fire. Others go to fetch Tamar, but she asks them to wait just a minute. For some reason, she thinks it would be a good idea to bring Judah's "stuff" to her trial. All of this paragraph is my interpretation, but I think it's pretty accurate.

When she is brought forth, she decides this would be a good time to show her evidence regarding the father of the child. I have this mental picture of men running into each other and falling down trying to put the fire out, especially Judah who is embarrassed beyond belief!

Tamar goes back home and has twin sons, Pharez and Zarah. Let's add this up.

- Judah leaves home, meets a wife, and gets married, 1 year.
- His wife has three sons, 3 years.
- Er grows up and gets married, 20 years.
- Er and Onan die. Same year? 1 year.
- Tamar waits for Shelah, 1 year.
- Tamar is pregnant, 1 year.
- Now we also know from Genesis 46:12 that Pharez grows up and gets married, 20 years.
- Pharez's wife has two sons who make the trip to Egypt, 2 years.

---

49 years.

So while "at that time" of Genesis 38:1 refers to Joseph's journey to Egypt, what happened at that time was the birth of Pharez. Pharez grew up, got married, and had two sons while Joseph was in Egypt. We know this because he shows up with two sons as Genesis 46:12 tells us.

Today's assignment: Don't just read the Bible and not understand what you're reading. Dig. If you don't have good extra biblical resources, ask someone who might know. God didn't inspire men to write stuff that isn't important. It's all important.

Do you think the Bible is important?_____

Pray God would give you wisdom to understand His Word.

Day 47

Read Genesis 45:6.
So the famine had been going on for two years. Let's add this up.

- Joseph gets sold to Potiphar at age seventeen. He gets out of prison after thirteen years. Thirteen.
- He is now thirty years old (Genesis 41:46). The seven years of plenty ended. Seven.
- Two years of famine go by before Joseph reveals his identity to his brothers. Two.

Twenty-two years
Joseph is now thirty-nine years old.

Look what Joseph says to his brothers (Genesis 45:7–8). He understands some of what God was doing in his life but not everything. He says, "God sent me before you to preserve you a posterity in the earth, and to save your lives by a great deliverance." That certainly happened, but that wasn't really what God was doing! Joseph goes on to say, "So now it was not you that sent me hither, but God; and he hath made me a father to Pharaoh, and lord of all his house, and ruler throughout all the land of Egypt." All of that part is certainly true. But why? What was God really doing?

I'm about to tell you something you won't like. It's this—you can look at any day in your Christian life and tell me what happened. What you can never tell me with certainty (and this is the part you won't like) is *why* it happened. The reason for this is because God doesn't need us to know why He is doing something. He only needs to have us do what he calls us to do and not be concerned with why. The why isn't our part. When we try to explain the "whys" of God's ways, we get it all wrong sometimes.

There was no way Joseph could possibly have known why all of this had happened to him. I know why, but Joseph would have had to live another 1,730 years to know. It certainly wasn't to save his brothers as he said in verse 7.

Today's assignment: You only need to know what God wants you to do and do it. You don't need to know *why*. What is God asking you to do?

_____
_____
_____
_____
_____

Pray that hearing what God asks you to do and doing it will satisfy your curiosity about life.

Day 48

Read Genesis 45:9, 47:13.

Joseph is thirty-nine when Jacob comes to Egypt. Jacob is 130 (Genesis 47:9). Benjamin could be as old as thirty-eight (one year younger than Joseph) but no younger than thirty because he has ten sons! (Genesis 46:21). Pharez is twenty-two, and his sons are close to two and one. Pharez's sons are Hezron and Hamul (Genesis 46:12).

Famines are natural disasters that take cruel tolls on human life. They are especially hard on three groups of humans. Sick people don't do well. Whether they are deteriorating or healing; the sick need excellent nutrition that is not available during a famine. Older people don't do well. Older people are running down in the best of conditions, and famines merely speed up that process. Finally, infants don't do well. Mother's milk dries up, parents become tired more easily without food, and infants receive less care and poorer nutrition than they need to survive. People die during famines—even healthy people. But the infirm, elderly, and young die at a much faster rate.

Today's assignment: Find a child between one and two years old. Ask around. Does that child need constant care and attention?

How would that child do with no food? How would he do with no one to care for him!

_____
_____
_____
_____
_____

Pray for those living through natural disasters. Pray that the Christians ministering to those affected by natural disasters can bring some to Christ.

Day 49

Read Genesis 3:1–15.
Read Luke 3:23.
Man's fall and God's solution. Wow! That's going back a bit! Both Adam and Eve disobeyed God in the Garden of Eden. God wasn't pleased with them and even less pleased with the serpent who had tricked them. God devised a plan right then to redeem fallen man. "And I will put enmity (antagonism) between thy seed and her seed" (Genesis 3:15). God began bringing the Messiah into the world right there in the beginning in the garden.

In Luke 3:23, the genealogy of Mary's side of Christ's family is given. Heli was Mary's father. Luke doesn't say Heli begat Joseph. He didn't. Joseph's biological father's name was Jacob (Matthew 1:16). Heli was Joseph's father-in-law. He was simply the legal father of Joseph.

The genealogies in Matthew 1 and Luke 3 are Christ's genealogies through both Joseph and Mary. Christ wasn't related to Joseph by blood, but even Joseph had a connection to David, Judah, Jacob, and Abraham as was prophesied for the Messiah.

Let's go to both of the genealogies and find out who is mentioned at the time of the famine while Joseph is in Egypt.

"And Judas (Greek for Judah) begat Phares (Greek for Pharez) and Zara (Greek for Zarah) of Thamar (Greek for Tamar) and Phares (Greek for Pharez) begat Esrom (Greek for Hezron)" (Matthew 1:3).

Then in Luke 3:33, it says, "Which was the son of Esrom which was the son of Phares, which was the son of Juda (another Greek form of Judah)."

So the Messianic bloodline that had started with Adam went through Hezron, who was brought to Egypt to live through the last five years of the famine which had hit Canaan. He was probably between one and two when he arrived. His father, Pharez, was twenty-two.

Today's assignment: Actually go to Matthew and Luke and read those genealogies. Understand that the Bible contains answers to questions. Do you have other questions? What are they?

_____
_____
_____
_____
_____

Dig in Scripture. It's a gold mine!

Pray. Thank God for His Word. It contains everything you need to know to get through life. Pray you won't neglect it.

Day 50

Now pay attention. This isn't spelled out in the Bible. This is just me using logic. For God to execute the plan he related to Satan in the Garden of Eden concerning the coming Messiah, He does not need Jacob—not at the time of the famine. Jacob could have died, and it wouldn't have thwarted God's plan one iota. That's because Jacob had already begotten Judah. God likewise didn't need Judah because Judah had already begotten Pharez of Tamar in chapter 38. God didn't need Pharez because Pharez had already begotten Hezron.

But Hezron was important! God needed to get food into Hezron. Hezron was the current end of the Messianic bloodline.

Jacob, Judah, Pharez, Joseph, Joseph's other brothers, Pharaoh, Potiphar, the butler, all the people mentioned by name between Genesis 37:1 and Genesis 46:11 could have died during the famine, and it would not have hindered God's plan for mankind. But not so with Hezron. Hezron needed to be kept alive until he became a father of the next link in the bloodline of Christ.

Today's assignment: Do you think it would be have been all right if Hezron had died in the famine? I mean, do you think God could have used Hamul, Hezron's brother? Or if they both had died, could God have started over? Be honest. What do you think?

_____
_____
_____
_____
_____

I'm a scientist. I think in terms of DNA, bloodlines, Punnett's squares, inherited traits, etc. Do you realize that if Hezron had died, there would have been no Boaz, Jesse, David, Solomon, no books of Psalms of David, no Proverbs of Solomon, no Ecclesiastes, Ruth, much of 1 and 2 Samuel, 1 and 2 Kings, 1 and 2 Chronicles, no Mary, no Joseph, and on and on. How about no Jesus? All the prophecies concerning Jesus in the Old Testament would not have had meaning.

Pray. Thank God for saving Hezron. Thank God for being so wise and so all seeing and so powerful.

Day 51

All along, you have thought this book and this Bible study was about Joseph. You did—admit it. You think your life is about you, where *you* go, what *you* study, who *you* marry, where *you* take your kids, how *you* deal with *your* problems, how God disciplines *you*, which sins easily tempt *you*, what kind of person *you* are. You think that I, this Bible study, God, Jesus, your family, your friends, all the places *you* go, and all the things around *you* are part of "*your* story." You do! I know you do. We all do. It's only natural.

We do the same thing with Bible characters. We think there is a different story about Adam, Noah, Abraham, Isaac, Jacob, Joseph, Moses, Joshua, David, and on and on. Well, there isn't! It's all one story.

I hate to pop your life's-all-about-me bubble, but it isn't about you at all! Joseph's story wasn't about him either. The story was more about Hezron than Joseph, and Hezron wasn't even mentioned in it! But it wasn't Hezron's story either. Don't you see?

The story is God's story about Jesus. Well, if it's God's story, why doesn't He exercise a little better control over it? I mean if it had been up to me, I would have prevented so many of the bad things. Jacob wouldn't have showed favoritism to Joseph. Joseph wouldn't have had those dreams. He wouldn't have gotten the coat. He wouldn't have been sold as a slave. Or if I came along later, I'd have gotten him out of prison long before Pharaoh's dream.

And Hezron would have died.

God is sovereign and does as He pleases. And thank goodness, His ways are not our ways (Isaiah 55:8). God does things perfectly.

Today's assignment: Is it a little scary thinking the story isn't about you? Tell the truth.

_____

_____

_____

_____

_____

Whatever you do, don't misconstrue that as God doesn't care about you. Nothing could be further from the truth! Pray that God would continue to reveal to you that you have nothing to fear. In spite of how things appear, God has every minute detail under control!

Day 52

    I haven't lived on the earth for very much of God's story. Oh, I know you all think more than seventy-six years is a long time, but it's not. There have been many natural disasters that I have seen in my life though. I've never seen God intervene to stop a natural disaster. He may have, but how would I know? Natural disasters happen all the time, and the ones that have happened in my life, God didn't stop. Earthquakes, tsunamis, storms, famines, droughts, floods—they have all happened, and God chose not to intervene. He didn't stop the famine that threatened to end the Messianic bloodline that would have occurred with the death of Hezron either. But God allowed the actions of men to bring about a good result in spite of the famine and in spite of some men's evil intentions.

    And here's the thing, and I don't want you to miss this. God gave every person, including Reuben, an opportunity to be part of the success of God's purpose! And guess who got to decide whether they would be part of that success? That's right! *They did!*

Today's assignment:
Do you think God has a plan?

_____

Who gets to decide whether you have a part in that plan?

_____

What is (are) your spiritual gift(s) (Romans 12:5–18, 1 Corinthians 12:7–11, Ephesians 4:11–12)?

_____
_____
_____
_____

How might you use your gift(s) in Christ's service?

_____
_____
_____
_____

How are you doing?

_____
_____
_____
_____

Who gets to decide how you are doing?

_____

Pray for God to reveal your gifts to you and show you clearly how to use them.

Day 53

Read Genesis 45:6–8.

Let's look more closely at what God says about what had happened to Joseph.

So God tells us by the hand of Moses that He "sent" Joseph to Egypt. But as we have shown, only Hezron needed to be spared. All the rest merely benefitted from what was happening to Hezron. Why Moses himself was a descendant of one of Levi's three sons (Exodus 2:1).

Well, how is all this related to you? Tell me, how do you see your life? Is your life complicated? Think about it. Have there been people in your life who have treated you unfairly? Have some even been mean to you? Have you been victimized by favoritism? Have you been victimized by jealousy? Have you ever been falsely accused of doing something you actually took a strong stand against? Have siblings ever lied to your parents about you? All those things happened to Joseph and yet he states, "God did send me before you to preserve life."

I can guess things about many of you. I know things about you that if someone heard it would make them cry. Those things make me cry. Many aspects of Joseph's life were like that. But none. (Are you listening?) *None* of those things in Joseph's life hindered God's plan! In fact, God used the horrible things in Joseph's life to *execute* His plan!

Favoritism, jealousy, slavery, false accusation, prison, being forgotten, twenty-two years separated from his family—*none of it hindered God!*

Today's assignment: What hinders God from bringing about His will for your life?

The answer? Only one thing. *Your attitude!*
Pray God will improve your attitude!

Day 54

We're not done.

"But you don't understand Duke. I have really suffered in life."

Then let's look at your life more closely and not talk about Joseph's problems. What are yours? Have you been overworked by a boss? Are you being overworked now? Have you been underpaid? Have supporters stopped sending money? Are you misunderstood at home? Are you homesick? Have you suffered punishment for the misbehavior of others? Are you underappreciated? Have you found yourself in jobs for which you have no talent? Have you been cut off by other drivers in traffic? Have you been splashed by a truck while walking as a pedestrian? Have you been rained on when you weren't prepared? Have you lost property in storms? In fires? Have you gone bankrupt? Have you lost money due to wrong speculation? Have you ever been sick? Are you still sick? Do you suffer from a debilitating disease? Are you disabled? Have you lost loved ones? Just what are your problems?

Well, tell me this. Just where was God when these things happened to you? Where was He? I'll tell you where He was. "And the Lord was with (Fill in Your Name.)"

Today's assignment: We're nearing the end of this study. I don't know if you did it one day at a time or all in one night. It doesn't matter.

Just know this, no matter how big your problems seem, God is right there with you. He has wanted you to go through this study so He could speak to you about you! Picture Him there behind you with His hand on your shoulder.

Pray. Thank God that He is so big that He's there with you and here with me on the farm in Georgia at the same time.

Day 55

You see, a story will one day be told about someone else. You will be in it. What part will you play? Will you be a good or a bad character in it? Will you be a jealous brother? Will you be a poor leader? Will you be a false accuser? Will you go through the story wondering where God is when you really need him? Or will the hand of God upon you be evident to everyone around you?

Guess what? You get to decide! No one else, not circumstances, not random events, not Satan, not any other thing determines whether others see the hand of God on your life. Only you do.

Today's assignment: What changes do you have to make in your behavior for others to see God's hand on your life?

_____
_____
_____
_____

Pray. It takes honesty and courage to make right changes in your life. Ask God for the honesty and courage you need to bring about those changes.

Day 56

Read Matthew 14:22–33.

In this passage, a storm came up on the Sea of Galilee. The disciples were in a ship being tossed in the waves and in danger of sinking. What I love about this story is that Jesus doesn't simply make the bad storm stop right away as He had done earlier (Mark 4:39). In this passage of Matthew, Jesus comes to the disciples, and He's walking on the water. The disciples were troubled and cried out for fear. Right away, Jesus comforts them by saying, "Be of good cheer, it is I, be not afraid."

You might relate your problems to me, and I might be impressed by the gravity of your situation. God isn't. You may be experiencing a storm in your life right now. Jesus visits us during storms. We don't always respond to His presence with joy. We are often troubled and cry out for fear. Jesus can bring calm.

It's one thing for a storm to stop. It's quite another for the sea to become calm. I was on an aircraft carrier in the South China Sea during a typhoon. Our escort ships looked like ping-pong balls in a bathtub full of three-year-olds. Even the carrier was rolling and listing pretty good. Then the word came that the storm was past. Well, I wish someone had told the South China Sea! They forgot. It didn't look any different to me when the storm stopped.

It's one thing for a storm to pass. It's quite another for the sea to be calm. Jesus can do both! He can do more. If you are willing to push away from everything worldly you trust in—nets, fish harvests, boats, sailing techniques, navigation methods—Jesus invites you to walk on the storms of your life.

Today's assignment: In what worldly things do you trust?

_____
_____
_____
_____
_____

Can they help you in the storms of life?

_____
_____
_____
_____
_____

Pray for courage in times of fear.
Pray for faith in times of doubt.
And it's okay to pray for the "sea to be still."

Day 57

So you're in a boat, sailing on the seas of life. A storm comes out of nowhere. Your brothers have thrown you in a pit. You hear them plotting your murder, then your sale as a slave. You can fear or trust.

The disciples were in a real boat in Matthew chapter 14. They had the same options you do. They could fear or trust. Most of them, for a long time afterward, only remembered a night on the sea when they were really scared. Peter alone trusted. For the rest of his life, he remembered walking on the water with Jesus.

The good news is, every one of those disciples went through other kinds of storms later in life. They all trusted Christ in those storms. He brought them courage, strength, peace, and calm.

God isn't absent from your life. He hasn't forsaken you. He is no less able to calm storms or protect you from famine than He was for Peter and Hezron. Don't forget Hezron. Not too many Christians have ever heard of Him.

Today's assignment: Maybe what appears to be a storm in your life has you in the bottom of the boat in fear. Are you huddled down there for some reason? Are you afraid?

_____
_____
_____
_____
_____

Pray that you will remember God saving Hezron. Pray you will remember Peter walking on the water. (I know it was ever so briefly, but he did it!) And pray God will rescue you from your fear.

Day 58

Isn't it time you stopped whining and complaining? If God directed Joseph's life in such a complicated way to bring about a good result, can't He work in yours? And what was that good result? *The redemption of mankind!*

And now you tell me God has abandoned you because He doesn't care about you? Does that make any sense at all? Don't you see how utterly ridiculous that is?

Then start acting like it!

Love in Christ,
Duke

About the Author

Duke Hammond was a captain in the United States Marine Corps. He flew helicopters in Vietnam. A near-death experience in the war led him on a two-year path to salvation. He has been married to Candy, the love of his life for fifty-three years, He is father of four Christian daughters married to four Christian sons-in-law. He is grandfather to eleven Christian grandchildren and great-grandfather to one. As a Christian, he has taught and preached Bible for nearly fifty years. He is an ordained minister of the gospel of Christ through The Missionary Church International. He cofounded 6:8 Ministries in 2005, a mission organization in Costa Rica, which is operating today.